A Guide to the Heavens

Early Modern Cultures of the Younger Europe

Volumes published in this Brill Research Perspectives title are listed at *brill.com/rpyes*

A Guide to the Heavens

The Literary Reception of Herman Hugo's
Pia desideria *in the Polish–Lithuanian Commonwealth*

By

Radosław Grześkowiak

BRILL

LEIDEN | BOSTON

Library of Congress Control Number: 2023921221

Typeface for the Latin, Greek, and Cyrillic scripts: "Brill". See and download: brill.com/brill-typeface.

ISSN 2950-4309
ISBN 978-90-04-54737-7 (paperback)
ISBN 978-90-04-54728-5 (e-book)
DOI 10.1163/9789004547285

Printed by Printforce, the Netherlands

Contents

Acknowledgements

I extend my heartfelt thanks to those whose generosity made the completion of this book possible. Special acknowledgment goes to Mirosława Hanusiewicz-Lavallee, Katarzyna Meller and Robert A. Maryks for choosing to include my work in their series and for their invaluable help in editing the translation. I am deeply appreciative of the warm Polish hospitality extended to me in London by my friends Małgorzata Broka and Tomasz Chabowski during my time at the Warburg Institute Library. I would also like to express my gratitude to Paul Hulsenboom for his substantial support in my research. For the English translation of the book, my thanks go to Józef Jaskulski.

I dedicate this book on the Polish versions of *Pia desideria* to my wife, Karolina, grateful for her understanding and patience.

Figures and Tables

Figures

Tables

A Guide to the Heavens

The Literary Reception of Herman Hugo's Pia desideria *in the Polish–Lithuanian Commonwealth*

Radosław Grześkowiak
Institute of Polish Philology, University of Gdańsk, Poland
radoslaw.grzeskowiak@ug.edu.pl

Abstract

This work discusses ten different translations and adaptations of Herman Hugo's emblem book *Pia desideria* (1624) in the Polish–Lithuanian Commonwealth. It shows how the engravings, elegies and exegetical extracts of the original volume were used by Polish-speaking authors. The author examines the reasons for the phenomenon of the volume's popularity and proves that it was determined by the interest of non-Latin speaking women.

Keywords

Herman Hugo – *Pia desideria* – Boëtius à Bolswert – religious emblem literature – Poland–Lithuania – Polish–Lithuanian Commonwealth – literary reception – artistic reception – engravings – elegies – exegesis – Old Polish literature

1 Introduction

This book is the first study on the reception of *Pia desideria* (Pious desires) in the Polish–Lithuanian Commonwealth, taking into account all known adaptations of the work written in Polish. First released in 1624, the concise volume by the Southern-Netherlandish Jesuit Herman Hugo (1588–1629)[1] had a staggering

---

1 Herman Hugo, *Pia desideria* (Antwerp: Hendrick Aertssens, 1624) (J.628/N.345). The successive editions of *Pia desideria* and its adaptations are identified in parentheses, numbered according to the following bibliographies: Peter M. Daly and G. Richard Dimler, *The Jesuit Series*, vol. 3 (Toronto: University of Toronto Press, 2002) (= J); Alison Adams, Stephen Rawles, and Alison Saunders, *A Bibliography of French Emblem Books of the Sixteenth and Seventeenth Centuries*, vols. 1–2 (Geneva: Librairie Droz, 1999–2000) (= F); John Landwehr, *German Emblem Books 1531–1888: A Bibliography* (Utrecht: A.W. Sijthoff, 1972) (= G); Landwehr, *Emblem*

career, becoming the most widely published emblem book of the seventeenth and eighteenth centuries. Its influence extended not only to Catholic countries but also to Lutheran, Calvinist, and Anglican ones, eventually reaching Orthodox Russia. When the volume went on sale, it is unlikely that anyone expected that it would make for the most popular and influential religious emblem book, in particular given the non-literary nature of Hugo's other works.

1.1   *A Bestseller out of the Blue*

The first publication penned by Hugo, a teacher of humanities at the Jesuit Antwerp college and subsequently the prefect of the Brussels college, was a scholarly treatise on the ancient book and the origins of writing, titled *De prima scribendi origine et universae rei litterariae antiquitate* (On the first origin of writing and on antiquity of all literature; 1617). His subsequent treatise, *De vera fide capessenda contra Balthasarum Meisnerum lutheranum et Henricum Brandium calvinistam* (On necessity to pursue the true faith, against Balthasar Meisner, a Lutheran, and Henricus Brandius, a Calvinist; 1620), was a religious polemic. During Hugo's tenure as the chief chaplain of the Spanish army in the Southern Netherlands, he published an account of the 1624–25 siege of Breda, *Obsidio Bredana armis Philippi III* (Siege of Breda by Philip III's forces; 1626); his posthumous publications include a study on the history of cavalry, *De militia equestri antiqua et nova* (On old and new cavalry; 1630), and a 1630 biography of the Italian Jesuit Carlo Spinola (1564–1622), who died a martyr's death in Japan. These publications show the impressive extent of the Jesuit's interests; however, none of them constituted a poetic volume[2] or had anything to do with emblems.

It is also worth remembering that the thoroughly considered and carefully crafted collection *Pia desideria* was written under difficult circumstances. Hugo penned it in 1621–23, during his few free moments en route to Madrid, where he traveled as a member of the retinue of the duke of Aerschot, Philippe-Charles d'Arenberg (1587–1640), and during his stint as the army chaplain.[3]

---

    and Fable Books Printed in the Low Countries 1542–1813: A Bibliography, 3rd ed. (Utrecht: HES, 1988) (= N); Paulina Buchwald-Pelcowa, *Emblematy w drukach polskich i Polski dotyczących XVI–XVIII wieku: Bibliografia* (Wrocław: Zakład Narodowy im. Ossolińskich, 1981) (= P).

2 Although Hugo likely influenced the final shape of an anthology of his students' poetry, *Fama postuma praesulum Antverpiensium, vulgata a Rhetoribus Collegii Soc[ietatis] Iesu eiusdem civitatis* (Posthumous fame of the prefect of the inhabitants of Antwerp, published by the rhetors of the college of the Society of Jesus of that city, 1611), no poem included in the collection bears his name.

3 See L[udovicus] van Miert, "Hugo Herman," in *Nieuw Nederlandsch biografisch woordenboek*, ed. Philip Christiaan Molhuysen, Petrus Johannes Blok, and Laurentius Knappert (Leiden: A.W. Sijthoff's Uitgevers-Maatschappij, 1921), 5:250–51; Mark Carter Leach, "The Literary and

Nonetheless, the work turned out to be a remarkable publishing success. The number of its reprints, translations, and adaptations leaves no doubt about that. By the middle of the seventeenth century alone, sixteen editions of *Pia desideria* had been published, followed by the same number in the next half-century, with at least another fourteen in the eighteenth century. And yet, the impressive number of reprints of this Latin work does not fully capture the magnitude of its success if one bears in mind its vivid vernacular reception.

The first wave of spirited interest in the newly published collection, illustrated with the striking copperplate engravings by Boëtius à Bolswert (*c.*1585–1633), occurred in the late 1620s and '30s. This was when the Latin editions of *Pia desideria* were joined by the first vernacular translations into national languages. The German translation by Benedictine monk Karl Stengel (1581–1663), *Gottselige Begirde* (J.727/G.359), was released in 1627, as was the French one, *Des pieux désirs*, signed with the initials "P.I." (J.701/F.334).[4] Shortly thereafter, Justus de Harduwijn's (1582–1636) translation into Dutch, *Goddelycke wenschen* (1629 [J.680/N.357]),[5] was released, followed by the publication of the Spanish edition, *Affectos divinos con emblemas sagradas* (Divine affections with sacred emblems; 1633 [J.768]), translated by the Jesuit Pedro de Salas (1584–1664).[6] In 1635, a Protestant adaptation by Francis Quarles (1592–1644) was published as part of a larger collection that lived to see eleven editions in merely half a century.[7]

The second wave of interest in the collection began to surge in the 1650s and continued until the 1680s. It was then that more translations and adaptations were released in German (at least eleven),[8] French (four), and Dutch (one),

---

Emblematic Activity of Herman Hugo, s.j. (1588–1629); A Dissertation" (PhD diss., University of Delaware, 1979), 1–108.

4 Agnès Guiderdoni-Bruslé and Aline Smeesters, eds., *Emblèmes et poésies des* Pieux désirs *de Herman Hugo* (*Anvers–Paris, 1627*) (Turnhout: Brepols, 2013). See Lynette C. Black, "Popular Devotional Emblematics: A Comparison of Sucquet's *Le chemin de la vie eternele* and Hugo's *Les pieux desirs*," *Emblematica* 9, no. 1 (1995): 1–20.

5 See Oscar Dambre, "Nabeschouwingen over *Pia desideria* (1624) en *Goddelijcke wenschen* (1629)," *Spiegel der Letteren* 2 (1958): 59–65.

6 See Pedro F. Campa, "The Spanish and Portuguese Adaptations of Herman Hugo's *Pia desideria*," in *Emblematic Perceptions: Essays in Honor of William S. Heckscher on the Occasion of his Ninetieth Birthday*, ed. Peter M. Daly and Daniel S. Russell (Baden-Baden: V. Koerner, 1997), 43–60.

7 Francis Quarles, Emblemes (*1635*) *and* Hieroglyphikes of the Life of Man (*1638*), ed. Karl Josef Höltgen and John Horden (Hildesheim: Georg Olms, 1993). See Karl Josef Höltgen, "Catholic Pictures versus Protestant Words? The Adaptation of the Jesuit Sources in Quarles's *Emblemes*," *Emblematica* 9, no. 1 (1995): 221–38.

8 See Michael Schilling, "'Der rechte Teutsche Hugo': Deutschsprachige Übersetzungen und Bearbeitungen der *Pia desideria* Hermann Hugos sj," *Germanisch-romanische Monatsschrift* 70 (1989): 283–300.

respectively. The period also marked the release of the first Italian translation by
Michele Cicogna (*fl.* 1678–83), titled *Fiamme d'Amor Divino dell'Anima desiderosa*
(Flames of divine love of the eager Soul; 1678 [J.750]), as well as José Pereira
Velosa's (1645–1711) translation into Portuguese, published as *Desejos piedosos*
(1687),[9] and Edmund Arwaker's (1665–1730) English version, *Pia desideria
or Divine Addresses* (1686 [J.689]).[10] At that time, the prints illustrating the
collection began to inspire painted decorations in the interiors and furnishings of both Catholic and Lutheran churches. It is worth remembering that
the copperplate illustrations in the successive editions of *Pia desideria* served
as a popular iconographic model not only in Europe but also in the continents
where Jesuit missionaries were active, primarily in South America.[11]

   Another tide of vernacular reception of *Pia desideria* took place in the first
half of the eighteenth century. French, German, and Dutch adaptations, tailored to the taste of the new era, were published at the time, including those
combining Hugo's collection with Otto van Veen's (1556–1629) volume *Amoris
Divini emblemata* (Divine love's emblems), such as *L'Ame amante de son Dieu*
(Soul loving its God; 1717 [J.694]) by Jeanne-Marie Bouvier de la Motte-Guyon
(1648–1717); an anonymous translation titled *Die ihren Gott liebende Seele* (Souls
loving their God; 1719 [J.743]); and a translation by the Mennonite Jan Suderman
(1680–after 1724), titled *De godlievende ziel* (God-loving soul; 1724 [J.684]). The
collection also ventured into new territories. In 1712, an anonymous Orthodox
Slavic adaptation, *Ifika jeropolitika* (The ethics of a holy citizen), was published
in Kyiv, illustrated with woodcuts by Nikodem Zubrzycki (d. *c.*1730), loosely
modeled on Bolswert's copperplate engravings, while 1718 saw the release of

9   See José Adriano de Freitas Carvalho, "As lágrimas e as setas: Os *Pia desideria* de Herman
       Hugo, s.j. em Portugal," *Via spiritus* 2 (1995): 169–201; Campa, "Spanish and Portuguese
       Adaptations."
10   See G. Richard Dimler, "Arwaker's Translation of the *Pia desideria*: The Reception of a
       Continental Jesuit Emblem Book in Seventeenth-Century England," in *The English Emblem
       and the Continental Tradition*, ed. Peter M. Daly (New York: AMS Press, 1988), 203–25;
       Anthony Raspa, "Arwaker, Hugo's *Pia desideria*, and Protestant Poetics," *Renaissance and
       Reformation* 24, no. 2 (2000): 63–74.
11   See, e.g., José Miguel Morales Folguera, "La celda del Padre Salamanca en el Convento
       de la Merced de Cuzco: Guia conceptual de la vida religiosa mercedaria en el altiplano
       peruano del setecientos," *Imago* 1 (2009): 79–97; Ricardo Estabridis, "Arte y vida mística:
       El alma y el amor divino en la pintura virreinal," *Revista del Museo Nacional* 50 (2010):
       129–55, here 135–51; Estabridis, "La cultura emblemática jesuita en una Casa de Ejercicios
       Espirituales para señoras limeñas," *Illapa* 8 (2011): 29–41, here 32–34.

the first Russian translation by Ivan Maximovich (c.1675–1732).[12] In turn, 1738 marked the publication of the Danish translation (J.678).

1.2 Current State of Research on Pia desideria

Although a substantial body of literature has been published on Hugo's volume and its reception, a number of issues have not been examined. The Latin text has not yet seen a scholarly edition with a commentary that would clarify the literary allusions in the elegiac texts, pinpoint filiations with ancient works,[13] or verify the accuracy of the exegetical excerpts attached to individual emblems. Modern-day editions generally follow the mold of phototype reproductions of an old print, with the scholarly apparatus limited to concise introductions.[14] In terms of accessibility and reproduction quality, editions of this type have now been surpassed by digital copies of old prints posted online.

Pia desideria has been the topic of several monographs. In an interesting amateur study from 1943, Pontianus (Pontien) Polman (1897–1968) et al. were the first to address the most important aspects of the volume, including its emblematic character and composition, the nature of the accompanying copperplates, as well as the poetics of the elegies and their meditative texture.[15] The other two monographs are dissertations centering on selected issues related to the collection and its author. Mark Carter Leach's 1979 study contains important findings on Hugo's life and scholarly pursuits while also discussing the structure and iconographic sources of nine selected emblems.[16]

---

12 See Сергей И. Николаев, "Литературные занятия Ивана Максимовича," *Труды Отдела древнерусской литературы* 40 (1985): 385–99. Although an early eighteenth-century Ukrainian translation of *Pia desideria* has also been reported (Walentyna Sobol, "Przekładowa literatura ukraińska w czasach późnego baroku," in *Translatoryka: koncepcje—modele—analizy: Księga jubileuszowa ofiarowana Profesor Barbarze Z. Kielar z okazji 80. rocznicy urodzin*, ed. Sambor Grucza et al. [Warsaw: UW 2010], 126), this is now known to be incorrect. The misunderstanding may have stemmed from Maximovich being of Ukrainian descent; however, his translation of Hugo's elegies was into Russian.

13 To be more precise: it has not seen them in the present, for an erudite compilation of such filiations was crafted by the rector of the Langensalza Lyceum, Johann Augustin Gröbel (*fl.* 1721–41), for the 1727 edition of *Pia desideria* (J.670).

14 Herman Hugo, *Pia desideria 1624*, ed. Hester M. Black (Menston: Scolar Press, 1971 [reprint of the first edition: J.628/N.345]); Hugo, *Pia desideria libri III*, ed. Ernst Benz (Hildesheim: Georg Olms Verlag, 1971 [reprint of the 1632 edition: J.636/N.347]).

15 Pontianus [Pontien] Polman et al., "De *Pia desideria* va pater Herman Hugo s.j. (1624)," supplement to: *Mons Alvernae* 18 (1942–43). I would like to extend my gratitude to Paul Hulsenboom for the opportunity to study the monograph.

16 Leach, "Literary and Emblematic Activity."

Conversely, Gabriele Dorothea Rödter's 1992 monograph focuses on the interplay of *Pia desideria*'s verbal and pictorial layers. Rödter demonstrates this relationship on the example of five emblems, which she analyzes in detail.[17] In turn, G. Richard Dimler's (1931–2020) 2003 publication summarizes the state of research on Hugo's collection and his life.[18]

Vernacular adaptations of the volume have attracted considerably more academic attention. Studies published on the subject typically analyze their relation to the original (I indicate major publications concerning this topic in the footnotes). What is striking, however, is the lack of monographs on the reception of *Pia desideria* in the literature (and fine arts) of the respective countries. One of the notable works that have paved the way for such research is Michael Schilling's discussion of the German adaptations of Hugo's work,[19] and a study on the Spanish and Portuguese adaptations by Pedro F. Campa.[20] The first comprehensive monograph of this kind is Feike Dietz's 2012 book on the interdenominational dissemination of *Pia desideria*'s religious substance in the seventeenth- and eighteenth-century Northern Netherlands.[21] The present book has been written from a similar academic perspective.

1.3 Polish Research on the Reception of Hugo's Collection

The process of integration of Hugo's volume in the Polish–Lithuanian state began with the arrival of the first copies of its early editions. The oldest known adaptations date back to 1657–71, that is, they were written during the second wave of the volume's popularity. It is worth noting that their appearance in the Polish–Lithuanian Commonwealth ran parallel to the artistic reception of *Pia desideria*'s engravings.[22] New translations were still being created in the

---

17 Gabriele Dorothea Rödter, *Via piae animae: Grundlagenuntersuchung zur emblematischen Verknüpfung von Bild und Wort in den* Pia desideria *(1624) des Herman Hugo s.J. (1588–1629)* (Frankfurt am Main: Peter Lang, 1992).

18 G. Richard Dimler, "Herman Hugo's *Pia desideria*," in Mundus emblematicus: *Studies in Neo-Latin Emblem Books*, ed. Karl A.E. Enenkel and Arnoud S.Q. Visser (Turnhout: Brepols, 2003), 351–79.

19 Schilling, "'Teutsche Hugo.'"

20 Campa, "Spanish and Portuguese Adaptations." Also noteworthy is the research conducted on the reception of prints in these editions, which inspired numerous *azulejos* (tileworks); see, e.g., João Pedro Monteiro's "Os *Pia desideria*, uma fonte iconográfica da azulejaria portuguesa do século XVIII," *Azulejo* 3/7 (1995/99): 61–70.

21 Feike Dietz, *Literaire levensaders: Internationale uitwisseling van woord, beeld en religie in de Republiek* (Hilversum: Verloren, 2012).

22 See, e.g., Monika Bubółka, "Przedstawienia wzorowane na dziele emblematycznym *Pia desideria* Hermana Hugona w polskiej sztuce nowożytnej" (M.A. thesis, Warsaw,

first half of the eighteenth century as part of the third wave of distinct interest in the book.

Polish literary historians have long been aware that Hugo's collection was of interest to Polish audiences, but it was not until recently that they have been able to recognize its full extent. Until the 1990s, only three Polish versions of *Pia desideria* from the seventeenth and eighteenth centuries were known: translations by Aleksander Teodor Lacki (1617–83) and Jan Żaba (1683–1754), and the emblematic collection by Zbigniew Morsztyn (*c*.1627–89). However, this knowledge was largely superficial. Lacki's translation was the subject of Bogusław Pfeiffer's (1960–2010) master's thesis, a part of which constituted the first publication devoted entirely to a Polish adaptation of *Pia desideria*.[23] Conversely, Żaba's translation has not been researched to this day. Only Morsztyn's emblems have received more attention, although their relationship to Hugo's volume has not yet been investigated.[24] Two of these adaptations, Lacki's and Morsztyn's, have been reprinted in the modern era, and while objections have been raised about their scholarly value,[25] both have contributed significantly to the upsurge in the research on the Polish editions of *Pia desideria*.[26]

UKSW, 2000); Marcin Wisłocki, "Hugo wędruje na wschód: Uwagi o recepcji *Pia desideria* Hermana Hugona w sztuce protestanckiej Europy Środkowej," *Quart* 15, no. 2 (2020): 17–33.

23   Bogusław Pfeiffer, "*Pobożne pragnienia* Aleksandra Teodora Lackiego: Pierwszy polski przekład utworu emblematycznego Hermana Hugona *Pia desideria*," *Ze skarbca kultury* 44 (1987): 9–52.

24   See, e.g., Hana Voisine-Jechova, "La visualisation ambiguë: Les emblèmes polonais de Morsztyn et leurs modèles," *Revue de littérature comparée* 64, no. 4 (1990): 689–703; Krzysztof Mrowcewicz, *Trivium poetów polskich epoki baroku: Klasycyzm—manieryzm—barok* (Warsaw: IBL, 2005), 217–56.

25   Aleksander Teodor Lacki, *Pobożne pragnienia*, ed. Krzysztof Mrowcewicz (Warsaw: Wydawnictwo IBL, 1997); see Peter M. Daly and G. Richard Dimler, "The New Edition of Herman Hugo's *Pia desideria* in Polish and Recent Hugo Scholarship," *Emblematica* 12 (2002): 351–60; Radosław Grześkowiak, "'Zwyczajem kawalerów ziemskich postępuje z nią Oblubieniec': Pierwotna dedykacja *Pobożnych pragnień* Aleksandra Teodora Lackiego jako autorski projekt lektury emblematów Hermana Hugona," *Pamiętnik literacki* 106, no. 1 (2015): 199–227, here 201, 206–8. Zbigniew Morsztyn, *Emblemata*, ed. Janusz and Paulina Pelc (Warsaw: Neriton, 2001); see critical comments in a review by Adam Karpiński, *Barok* 9, nos. 1/2 (2002): 213–15.

26   See, e.g., Joanna Hałoń, "W poszukiwaniu źródeł inspiracji, czyli o dwóch polskich wersjach *Pia desideria* Hermana Hugona," *Roczniki humanistyczne* 50, no. 2 (2002): 127–60; Feike Dietz, Els Stronks, and Katarzyna Zawadzka, "Rooms-katholieke *Pia desideria*: Bewerkingen in internationaal perspectief," *Internationale Neerlandistiek* 47, no. 3 (2009): 31–49.

A true outpour of information concerning the hitherto unknown literary adaptations began at the turn of the twentieth century and continues to this day. An anonymous adaptation of *Pia desideria* was discovered in 1992.[27] More than a decade later, it was identified as the work of Mikołaj Mieleszko (1607–67). A copy of a second version of this collection bearing the author's name was discovered in St. Petersburg. This led to the publication of a critical edition of Mieleszko's version in 2010.[28] Source queries conducted in connection with the release of said edition resulted in the discovery of two minor poetic pieces related to Hugo's emblems: a poetic annotation on a printed copy of the engraving to the emblem II, 5,[29] and an anonymous translation of elegy III, 6.[30] The 2010s have produced further revelations: three adaptations of *Pia desideria* were discovered in the manuscript collections of Discalced Carmelite convents in Poland, and another copy of one of these adaptations was found in Lviv. All three works were published in a critical edition with extensive commentary in 2020.[31]

In a relatively short period of time, the number of Old Polish adaptations of Hugo's emblem book has risen from three to ten, with the dynamic nature of the new discoveries suggesting that the full scope of the adaptations created in the Polish–Lithuanian Commonwealth has yet to be revealed. A substantial part of the recent finds comprises items preserved in monastic book collections. Since the latter have been understudied in Poland, they may still hold a number of undisclosed testimonies concerning the reception of *Pia desideria*.

---

27   Stanisław Szczęsny, "*Pia desideria* Hermana Hugona w bibliotece benedyktynek sando-
      mierskich: Nieznany przekład polski," in *Literatura polskiego baroku w kręgu idei*, ed. Alina
      Nowicka-Jeżowa, Mirosława Hanusiewicz, and Adam Karpiński (Lublin: Wydawnictwo
      KUL, 1995), 161–65, here 163–65.

28   Mieleszko Mikołaj, *Emblematy*, ed. Radosław Grześkowiak and Jakub Niedźwiedź (Warsaw:
      Neriton, 2010).

29   Radosław Grześkowiak and Jakub Niedźwiedź, "Unknown Polish Subscriptions to the
      Emblems of Otto van Veen and Herman Hugo: A Study on the Functioning of Western
      Religious Engravings in the Old-Polish Culture," *Terminus: Special Issue* 1 (2019): 1–29.

30   Radosław Grześkowiak, "'Po różnych królestwach i prowincyjach Dusza nabożna szukała
      kochanka swego': Stratyfikacja staropolskiej recepcji jezuickich druków emblematycznych
      na przykładzie *Pia desideria* Hermana Hugona," in *Kultura Pierwszej Rzeczypospolitej w
      dialogu z Europą: Hermeneutyka wartości*, vol. 6, *Formowanie kultury katolickiej w dobie
      potrydenckiej*, ed. Justyna Dąbkowska-Kujko (Warsaw: Wydawnictwo UW, 2016), 249–99,
      here 295–99.

31   Radosław Grześkowiak, Jolanta Gwioździk, and Anna Nowicka-Struska, *Karmelitańskie
      adaptacje* Pia desideria *Hermana Hugona z XVII i XVIII w.* (Warsaw: Neriton, 2020).

1.4   *Study Concept and Layout*

The popularity of Hugo's volume in the Polish–Lithuanian Commonwealth is a phenomenon that any other emblem book has not matched. The collection *Emblematum libellus* (Little book of emblems) by Andrea Alciato (1492–1550) was not fully translated into Polish between the sixteenth and eighteenth centuries, with as few as four poets attempting to adapt a significant number of Alciato's epigrams. Among Polish readers, religiously themed emblem books were noticeably more popular than humanist collections. Some of the titles that are considered as popular at the time—on account of each seeing two Polish translations by the end of the eighteenth century—include the diptych *Paradisus Sponsi et Sponsae* (Paradise of Bridegroom and Bride) by the Jesuit Jan David (1546–1613) and *De aeternitate considerationes* (Reflections on eternity) by another Jesuit, Jeremias Drexel (1581–1638). Another highly popular work was the graphic cycle *Cor Iesu amanti sacrum* (Heart dedicated to Jesus's love), crafted around 1600 by Anton II Wierix (*c.*1555–1604); it lived to see four adaptations in Polish. Against this backdrop, the literary reception of *Pia desideria*, which consists of ten different adaptations (including the three that were edited by different authors), seems rather impressive.

That Hugo's volume was indisputably the most popular Western emblem book in the Polish–Lithuanian state makes its reception a worthy subject of a case study that would illuminate the most important mechanisms of dissemination, integration, and assimilation of such Latin collections in Poland-Lithuania. The importance of such a project is all the greater because aside from the aforementioned Dietz study, whose nature is somewhat different, there is a palpable lack of monographic studies on the overall reception of *Pia desideria* in the writing and culture of the respective countries in which it was read.

This monograph focuses on the literary echoes of Hugo's collection. The analysis spans all known adaptations, regardless of whether they comprised a complete reworking of all emblems in the collection or just one. Throughout the study, I apply philological methods, to a large extent organizing and correcting the findings of my predecessors. Wherever possible, I also try to identify the edition that served as the basis for a given adaptation. This is because researchers of vernacular versions of *Pia desideria* sometimes trace them directly to the first edition (which is the best known today), drawing far-reaching conclusions about the nature of a given adaptation based on discernible discrepancies between them. However, since the Latin version took different typographic forms, pointing out the correct one prevents this methodological error from being perpetuated.[32]

---

32   See Raspa, "Arwaker," 63–64; Dietz, *Literaire levensaders*, 43.

The adopted holistic perspective enables a new perspective on the subject. Only then is it possible to demonstrate the full extent and significance of *Pia desideria*'s influence on the religious literature of the Polish–Lithuanian state and to document how this volume's audience expanded by including lay readers, representatives of different denominations and women, as manifested in other countries.[33] The monographic scope also allows me to highlight the peculiarities of the Polish adaptations and distinguish the most important interpretations of Hugo's emblem book.

In the first Part of this monograph, I outline the solutions adopted in *Pia desideria* that were vital to the book's popularity. I also analyze the reception of the Latin volume in the Polish–Lithuanian lands, which points to the tendency to penetrate through confessional barriers. My goal is to demonstrate that the plethora of Polish adaptations was the result of women's unfamiliarity with Latin, and that these adaptations helped overcome the greatest barrier to the widespread reception of Hugo's volume—the barrier of gender.

Hugo's volume was never translated into Polish in its entirety. Out of the elements of the original emblems, Polish authors would choose those that best suited their sensibilities and interests. Hence, I have divided my analysis of individual adaptations into three Parts, the first of which covers the versions centered on the engravings (I have also briefly presented their artistic reception in the Polish–Lithuanian Commonwealth and the neighboring countries); the second deals with the translations of the elegies; and the third with the adaptations of excerpts from exegetical works complementing the forty-five emblems that comprise *Pia desideria*.

In the last Part of the book, I identify the most important models of reception, to which the respective Polish adaptations of *Pia desideria* were tailored. These include meditative reading, exegetical reading, and artistic reading, as well as framing the work as a spiritual romance. This Part also discusses the influence of handwritten and printed literary circulation on the reach of individual adaptations (extensive in the case of printed works; singular in the case of transcripts).

A combined examination of all adaptations of *Pia desideria* allows for a multifaceted analysis of the assimilation of Hugo's bestselling emblem book into the Polish language, while also indicating the type of content that Polish and Lithuanian audiences sought therein for nearly one and a half centuries.

---

33   No Polish adaptations for young readers are known to exist. See Feike Dietz, "*Pia desideria* through Children's Eyes: The Eighteenth-Century Revival of *Pia desideria* in a Dutch Children's Book," *Emblematica* 17 (2009): 191–212; Dietz, *Literaire levensaders*, 262–302.

2 *Pia desideria*: The Anatomy of Success

2.1 *A Formula for a Bestselling Emblem Book with a Religious Theme*

In early 1531, a collection of illustrated epigrams by the Italian jurist and humanist Andrea Alciato was first published in Augsburg, followed by its first authorized edition, entitled *Emblematum libellus*, released three years later in Paris. Numerous revivals of this volume sparked the rise of a new genre that interlocked a literary text with a graphic representation of the underlying theme. Members of the Society of Jesus began to take a keen interest in emblems from as early as the mid-sixteenth century, recognizing the genre as an attractive and hence useful tool for molding ethical behavior and enhancing piety.[34] Teaching the principles of emblematic writing in Jesuit colleges was sanctioned by the *Ratio studiorum* (Plan of studies). In line with its guidelines, students were to be trained in writing emblems on an assigned topic, with exemplary works showcased publicly, hung out in prominent places together with the accompanying prints. The codification of teaching practices resulted in the exponential growth of Jesuit emblem collections in the early decades of the seventeenth century.[35]

The most popular and acclaimed emblem book by a Jesuit author in the seventeenth and eighteenth centuries was the collection *Pia desideria*, first published in 1624. Before proceeding to discuss its popularity in the Polish–Lithuanian Commonwealth, it is important to outline some of the key features that turned the collection into a bestseller.

2.1.1 Erotic Origins

At a time when Jesuit emblematic writing was still seeking the most effective forms of expression, a remarkable wave of erotically-themed emblems swept through the Low Countries. It began in 1601 with the printing of a collection whose authorship is attributed to the Leiden professor of poetics and Greek Daniël Heinsius (1580–1655). Most of the engravings here showed Cupid

---

34 See, e.g., G. Richard Dimler, "Jesuit Emblem Books: An Overview of Research Past and Present," in *Emblem Studies in Honour of Peter M. Daly*, ed. Michael Bath, Pedro F. Campa, and Daniel S. Russell (Baden-Baden: V. Koerner, 2002), 63–122.

35 See, e.g., G. Richard Dimler, "A Bibliographical Survey of Emblem Books Produced by Jesuit Colleges in the Early Society: Topography and Themes," *Archivum historicum Societatis Iesu* 48 (1979): 297–309; Paulina Buchwald-Pelcowa, "Emblematyka w polskich kolegiach jezuickich," in *Artes atque humaniora: Studia Stanislao Mossakowski sexagenario dicata*, ed. Andrzej Rottermund et al. (Warsaw: Instytut Sztuki PAN, 1998), 169–79.

focused on various activities, supplied with poetic captions that inspired moralistic interpretations. Reissued in 1608 under the title *Emblemata amatoria* (Love emblems), the volume became a template for a number of imitators. In the first decades of the seventeenth century, it was joined by the anonymous *Theatre d'amour* (Theater of love; *c.*1606); *Amorum emblemata* (Emblems of loves; 1608) by Otto van Veen; *Emblemata amatoria* (Love emblems; 1611) by Pieter Corneliszoon Hoft (1581–1647); *Thronus Cupidinis sive Emblemata amatoria* (Cupid's throne or love emblems; *c.*1616) by Crispijn de Passe the Elder (1564–1637); and *Emblemata amoris* (Emblems of love; 1622) by Raphael Custos (1590–1664). Most of these collections had reprints, reworkings, and continuations, ensuring the enduring success of erotic emblems throughout the century.

Given the subject under discussion, the most interesting among these copiously produced pieces is the volume by the noted painter and printmaker van Veen and its subsequent history. When van Veen's *Amorum emblemata* found its way into the hands of Isabella Clara Eugenia (1566–1633), the governor of the Southern Netherlands, renowned for her piety, the future Poor Clare pointed out that if Cupid were to be replaced by the Divine Love, then the erotic volume—attuned to the needs of holy love—would be elevated from a carefree book to the status of an engaging catechetical lesson.[36] Van Veen heeded Isabella's advice and refashioned his erotic collection into a book that became the apotheosis of the Divine Love. This led to the publication of the 1615 volume *Amoris Divini emblemata* (Emblems of the divine love), in which the metaphysical romance of the Soul and the Divine Love is dissected into sixty emblems. In the engravings, the Soul is depicted as a several-year-old girl, barefoot, equipped with a pair of wings, wearing a ragged ankle-length robe tied at the waist, her hair pinned up in a bun. Conversely, the Divine Love is depicted as her male peer clad in a shorter, knee-length robe, winged and with a nimbus around his head, carrying the unmistakable bow and a quiver full of arrows. To dispel any doubt about who they represent, the artist captioned both figures "Anima" and "Amor Divinus," respectively, in the very first illustration in which they appear.[37] The young age of the protagonists implies that, despite their entanglement in a passionate relationship, the erotic nature of their bond could be softened and infantilized. Focused on a personal religious experience, the cycle appealed with extraordinary power to the collective imagination of the era, launching a series of numerous emblem books dedicated to the couple.

---

36   Otto van Veen, *Amoris Divini emblemata* (Antwerp: Martin Nuyts, 1615), 4.
37   Van Veen, *Amoris Divini emblemata*, 11.

Van Veen also changed the authors from whom he drew the Latin inscriptions. The *Amorum emblemata* collection included quotations from writers of Greco-Roman antiquity, most notably Ovid (43 BCE–17/18 CE), Seneca the Younger (4 BCE–65 CE), Plutarch (*c*.46–after 119), Propertius (*c*.50–after 15 BCE), Virgil (70–19 BCE), Cicero (106–43 BCE), Tibullus (*c*.54–19 BCE), and Publilius Syrus (*fl.* first century BCE). Using florilegia of the likes of *Polyanthea nova* (New polyanthea; 1604),[38] van Veen replaced inscriptions with quotations from the Bible and from the writings of the doctors of the church, including first and foremost St. Augustine of Hippo (354–430), followed by the far less frequently featured quotes from St. Bernard of Clairvaux (1090–1153), St. Gregory the Great (*c*.540–604), and St. Jerome of Stridon (331/47–420).

Van Veen's solutions were received with enthusiasm by admirers of devotional literature. They were also adapted for use in the *Pia desideria* volume by Hugo, who borrowed from his predecessor the pair of main protagonists and their erotic relationship. And while one can search in vain in Hugo's elegies for any mention that the personifications of the Soul and the Divine Love take a childlike form, the printmaker Bolswert patterned the representations of both characters on van Veen's copperplates.[39] Hugo directly explained this arrangement in one of his elegies, stating that Cupid would not have conquered the world if he had not been a little boy, since it is children of his age who are most loved by all (II, 9, vv. 21–24). Bolswert's alterations are limited to stripping the image of the Soul of its wings (they appear only incidentally, on the illustrations accompanying emblems III, 9 and 13, as deemed fit by the biblical inscription), while the Divine Love is seen missing its bow and arrows (in engraving II, 1, they are depicted as Cupid's attributes).[40]

Unlike the engravings in the *Amoris divini emblemata* collection, the personifications in the engravings to *Pia desideria* were not captioned. As a result, the

---

38   Jan Bloemendal, "Een emblematicus en zijn inspiratie: De bronnen van Otho Vaenius' *Amoris divini emblemata*, Antwerpen 1615; Ontlening en adaptie," *Tijdschrift voor Nederlandse Taal-en Letterkunde* 118 (2002): 273–87.

39   See, e.g., Mario Praz, *Studies in Seventeenth-Century Imagery* (Rome: Edizioni di Storia e Letteratura: 1975), 1:35–8, 146–47; Leach, "Literary and Emblematic Activity," 114–19.

40   In this study of *Pia desideria*, I use Roman numerals to designate the number of a book, and Arabic numerals to refer to the number of a given piece in the book, while also listing the introductory emblem as zero (0). Such numeration was only introduced in the 1628 edition published by Hendrik van Haestens of Leuven (J.633), followed by its adoption in the subsequent reissues. In the original 1624 version (J.628/N.345) and in several early editions, the introductory emblem bears no number, while the others were numbered from one to forty-five, independent of the books (the original numeration corresponded with Bolswert's designation of copperplates from zero to forty-five).

identification of the saintly child with the Divine Love was not at all obvious to the recipients of Hugo's volume. This also applies to Polish translations and adaptations, in which the figure was identified as the Divine Love or Jesus. Significantly, when a Polish reader labeled the main characters on the engraving accompanying emblem 1, 1 in their copy of *Pia desideria*, they labeled the girl with the inscription "Anima," without adding any caption next to the boy.[41]

The feeling that united the two protagonists in van Veen's 1615 collection thus appears as subdued and balanced. Inspired by the bridal mysticism derived from the Song of Songs, Hugo's elegies substantially amplify the gamut of the underlying emotions and desires. This change was one of the many fortuitous solutions behind the innovative concept that ensured the volume such tremendous success.

2.1.2   Emblem Composition: Inscriptions

The very title *Pia desideria emblematis, elegiis et affectibus s[anctorum] patrum illustrata* (Pious desires illustrated with emblems, elegies, and affections of the holy fathers) points to the author's concept concerning the composition of the individual pieces comprising the collection (fig. 1). Each of them consists of four parts. The most important one is a biblical quotation that underpins and captions the other three elements: an illustration (by Hugo, according to the custom of the era, referred to as an emblem); an extensive elegy; and excerpts from the works of the doctors of the church, comprising an exegetical commentary on the biblical verse and the issues it addresses.

The verses selected by Hugo as emblem inscriptions were by no means chosen accidentally. The largest group of quotations comes from the book of Psalms (23). In the first book of *Pia desideria*, which is penitential in nature, the eloquence of the respective pieces is amplified by the bitter verses from the book of Job (5), while in the middle of the second book, when the Soul, freed from the yoke of sins, strives to master the Christian virtues, it is captioned with the verses from the Song of Songs (13). In addition, Hugo cites one verse each from Deuteronomy, the prophetic books of Isaiah and Jeremiah, and two of St. Paul's epistles (Romans and Philippians).

---

41   Herman Hugo, *Pia desideria* (Milan: Giovan Battista Bidelli, 1634) (J.637), 24 (Jagiellonian Library, call no. Teol. 4802 I). The iconographic code, understandable to users of religious emblem books from under the sign of bridal love in the seventeenth and eighteenth centuries, had become obscure by the nineteenth century. The author of the 1843 Polish paraphrase of *Pia desideria* had trouble identifying the male figure, labeling him as an angel or, possibly, as God (Herman Hugo, *Pobożne pragnienia*, trans. Bonifacy Ostrzykowski [Warsaw: Księża Misjonarze, 1843], vii).

FIGURE 1   Boëtius à Bolswert, frontispiece in: Herman Hugo, *Pia desideria* (Antwerp: Hendrik Aertssens, 1624), engraving. Amsterdam, Rijksmuseum

The quotations were selected for their strong emotional appeal. This is especially true of verses from the Psalms of David, Song of Solomon, Job's Complaint,
and the prophetic books. Most of them pose dramatic questions (e.g., "Why
turnest thou thy face away and forgettest our want and our trouble?" [Ps. 43:24;
I, 7]) or commands (e.g., "Bring my soul out of prison, that I may praise thy
name!" [Ps. 141:8; III, 10]).[42] In all quotations, the speaking subject appears in
the first person singular so that the reader can more easily identify with the
speaker. Together, the quotations add up to the eponymous "pious desires" (*pia
desideria*), elaborated comprehensively in the other elements of each emblem.
These verses are the cornerstone of the entire collection, which expounds on
the tenets of inner piety that—contrary to doctrinal rigorism—underscores a
fervent and individualized experience of the truths of faith.

The choice of paragraphs whose appeal is primarily emotional rather
than intellectual, was a key innovation of Hugo's religious collection. It was
strongly emphasized by the frontispiece that advertised the volume. The copperplate features silhouettes of five biblical authors, David with a lyre, Paul
the Apostle in prayer, Daniel among lions, Moses with the stone tablets, and
Jeremiah with a book. Each is accompanied by a verse from a book of their
respective authorship. These quotations correspond with the inscriptions in
the emblems, a form in which nearly all of them recur throughout the volume,
complemented at the illustrative, elegiac, and exegetical levels. David is accompanied by the inscription from emblem III, 11; emblem III, 9 corresponds with
St. Paul; emblem I, 14 with Moses; emblem I, 8 with Jeremiah. Only Daniel, captioned on the frontispiece with the verse "Daniel, vir desideriorum" (Daniel,
thou man of desires; Dan. 10:11), is referred to in the collection with the name-
less designation of "Medus puer" in elegy I, 12 (v. 29). The verses of the eponymous copperplate directly articulate the desires addressed to God, joining in
a concerted chorus of the titular pious yearnings. Their character is emphasized by the cordial backdrop of the engraving: a blazing heart fitted with a pair
of wings that elevate it toward the divine object of love. Upon closer inspection, one notices a number of dramatic questions and exclamations written
on the individual feathers of both wings. For those who interact with emblem
literature on a daily basis, reading this iconographically condensed engraving, and thus reconstructing the message of the collection, must have posed
no difficulty.

The verses selected as emblem inscriptions were familiar to the prospective readers of the book. Little is currently known about the praying habits of
laypersons in early modern times; far more research exists on the inner life of

---

42   Translations from the Vulgate and verse numbering after the Douay–Rheims Translation.

nuns, who, encouraged by their confessors, turned to writing spiritual auto-
biographies, edifying prayers, or songs that glorified God. In the seventeenth-
century Polish–Lithuanian Commonwealth, Discalced Carmelite nuns created
hundreds of devotional songs for their own use, which they later copied in manuscript songbooks. A number of devotional exclamations that Hugo adapted
from the book of Psalms or the Song of Songs, turning them into emblematic
inscriptions, can also be found in the anonymous songs by Carmelite nuns.[43]
The community of biblical sites linking the Dutch emblematic collection with
the songs and prayers of Polish Carmelite nuns shows the extent to which the
verses selected as inscriptions by Hugo constituted *loci communes* (commonplaces) for early modern prayers. Their widespread familiarity largely contributed to the popularity of the collection.

2.1.3   Emblem Composition: Engravings
Significant to the success of the volume were its attractive engravings. They
were crafted by Bolswert, one of Antwerp's most talented copperplate engravers, master of the Guild of St. Luke, a close associate of Peter Paul Rubens (1577–
1640), as well as a functionary of the Jesuit sodality, famous for his illustrations
to other devotional bestsellers, including *Via vitae aeternae* (The path of eternal life; 1620) by Antoine Sucquet (1574–c.1627) and *Schola cordis* (The school of
heart; 1629) by Benedictus van Haeften (1588–1648).[44] The author of illustrations
to *Pia desideria* is indicated by an annotation on the title page of the first engraving, which reads, "Vulgavit Boëtius a Bolswert" (Published by Boëtius a Bolswert).
The copperplate engravings are not signed, but one of them contains a depiction
of the Soul resting on an earth globe that marks several major urban centers in
the Low Countries: Brussels, Antwerp, Mechelen, 's-Hertogenbosch, Utrecht, and
Amsterdam, as well as the small Frisian municipality of Bolsward—Boetius's
hometown—indicated in the corner of the engraving (III, 6).

   In the early seventeenth century, engravings illustrating religiously themed
emblem books relied on several different conventions. *Devises heroïques* (Heroic
mottoes) by the French canon Claude Paradin (1512–73) popularized emblems
of a heraldic character. Jacob Cats's (1577–1660) collection *Sinne-en minne-
beelden* (Portraits of morality and love) came out supplied with engravings
featuring realistic genre scenes, which only acquired religious significance

43   Radosław Grześkowiak, Jolanta Gwioździk, and Anna Nowicka-Struska, *Karmelitańskie
      adaptacje* Pia desideria *Hermana Hugona z XVII i XVIII w.* (Warsaw: Neriton, 2020), 20–26.
44   Marie Chévre, "*Pia desideria* illustrés par Boëce de Bolswert," *Gutenberg Jahrbuch* 41
      (1966): 291–99; Ernst Thomas Reimbold, "*Geistlische Seelenlust*: Ein Beitrag zur barocken
      Bildmeditation; Hugo Hermann, *Pia Desideria*, Antwerpen 1624," *Symbolon: Jahrbuch für
      Symbolforschung* N.F. 4 (1978): 93–161.

when interpreted in a specific way. Subordinated to meditative purposes, Jesuit emblem books employed several popular illustrative strategies. The first one involved allegorical scenes whose meaning became clear when reading the poetic caption, as is the case with the copperplates in Drexel's *De aeternitate considerationes*. The second strategy relied on engravings made up of several planes supplemented with letter designations referring to the relevant excerpt in the text, as is the case in *Adnotationes et meditationes in Evangelia* (Annotations and meditations on the Gospels) by Jerónimo Nadal (1507–80). One variation of such cross-referenced engravings were simultaneous allegorical compositions composed of several temporal and spatial planes, such as *Paradisus Sponsi et Sponsae* by the Jesuit Jan David (1546–1613) or *Via vitae aeternae* by Sucquet. When developing his engravings for the *Pia desideria* collection, however, Bolswert did not use any of the aforementioned strategies. His main inspiration came from van Veen's illustrations for *Amoris Divini emblemata*.

Bolswert's borrowings from van Veen are not limited to the pair of main protagonists but also include the way in which the respective scenes are arranged, pinpointing the interaction between the characters against the background of a landscape, less often an interior. The symbolic significance here lies in the presented scene (e.g., the Divine Love illuminates the path of the Soul in the darkness, the Divine Love is concealed from the Soul behind a veil). Those Polish adaptations that also included brief descriptions of the respective engravings prove that, regardless of the denominational differences between their authors, they had no difficulty in interpreting the novel iconographic solutions.

Apparently, Bolswert only went against this compositional principle on one occasion, in the engraving of emblem I, 15, where he multiplied beyond measure the symbols meant to make up the complex significance of the scene depicted. With her final breath, the personification of the Soul utters a cry, "Eheu!" (Alas!). This is the only instance in the entire series in which an engraving contains a statement presented in the form of a proto-speech balloon. The girl's head rests on a sheaf of hay (an allusion to the biblical figure of the passing of life) or myrrh (a symbol of mortality), accompanied by a shattered winged hourglass that has fallen out of her hand (the wings symbolize the celerity of time, while the breaking of the hourglass stands for the end of human existence). In the background, two girls walk away in opposite directions—one of them carries the Sun on her head while the other holds the Moon (personifications of day and night, respectively); an old man hovers above them, equipped with a scythe and an hourglass placed on her head (it is Time portrayed as Saturn). This exception shows the avenue that could have been explored by the iconographic design of the volume, one that drew close to the symbol- and narrative-laden simultaneous engravings developed by Bolswert for Sucquet's volume four years earlier. Nevertheless, the artist settled on simple depictions whose suggestiveness resulted in them being eagerly imitated in subsequent book engravings (some of which illustrated the Dutch translation of the Bible or the reissue of Ignatius of Loyola's [c.1491–1556] *Spiritual Exercises*)[45] and helps account for their great popularity as attractive themes in sacral painting from the mid-seventeenth century onward.

The pair of child protagonists portrayed in the engravings has no equivalent in Hugo's elegies. The main inspiration for such depictions came from van Veen's engravings. And yet, there are many indications that both the scenes shown in the individual copperplates and the accompanying props were the invention of Hugo himself. This conclusion is prompted by the nature of engravings in Hugo's other prints, which each time had to be developed strictly according to his instructions, whether they were depictions of various figures of the ancient book in the treatise *De prima scribendi origine et universae rei literariae antiquitate*, plans and diagrams of fortifications in the print *Obsidio Bredana*, or diagrams of complex equestrian formations in the cavalry treatise *De militia equestri antiqua et nova*. Hugo's authorship is also indicated by the close correlation of the details in the engravings developed for *Pia desideria* (e.g., supporting scenes) with the poetic comparisons in the elegies or the themes present in the exegetical paragraphs compiled by Hugo.

For the sake of the *Pia desideria* prints, Hugo and Bolswert succeeded in annexing iconographic schemes that had gained popularity in secular emblem books. A notable example is the engraving of emblem III, 9, which shows a winged Soul reaching out toward the heavens, its leg chained to a *globus cruciger*.[46] In this instance, the symbol of power over the world serves as a visible sign of wordly authority, which in the spiritual plane turns into a ball and chain (fig. 2). The scene constitutes a reference to an emblem by the genre's originator, Alciato. The same plane features an illustration for the epigram *Paupertatem summis ingeniis obesse, ne provehantur* (Poverty prevents the advancement of the best of abilities) in his *Emblematum libellus*, with the image of God in the upper corner of the engraving. It depicts a boy with one

45 Ralph Dekoninck, "The Circulation of Images," in Emblemata sacra: *Emblem Books from the Maurits Sabbe Library, Katholieke Universiteit Leuven*, ed. Ralph Dekoninck, Agnès Guiderdoni-Bruslé, and Marc van Vaeck (Philadelphia: Saint Joseph's University Press, 2006), 31–36.

46 Praz, *Studies in Seventeenth-Century Imagery*, 35–38, 146–47; Lubomír Konečný, "The Rise and Fall of a Hero," in *Impossible Heroes: Icarus and Phaeton as the Emblematic Figures of Modern Man*, ed. Eva Bendová et al. (Prague: Národní galerie, 2020), 15–36.

Coarctor autem è duobus; desiderium habens dissolui et esse cum Christo. Ad Philip. 1.

39.

FIGURE 2 Boëtius à Bolswert, engraving no. 39 (III, 9) in: Herman Hugo, *Pia desideria* (Antwerp: Hendrik Aertssens, 1624). Amsterdam, Rijksmuseum

hand weighted down by a stone, and the other, winged one, soaring toward the sky.[47]

In the sixteenth and seventeenth centuries, Alciato's emblem enjoyed great popularity in students' albums as an ornament to entries made by indigent students.[48] When in 1618 Jacob van der Heyden (1573–1645) compiled a collection of engravings intended as an *album amicorum* (album of friends; i.e., an early form of friendship book) for students, he included a copperplate portraying an elegant youth with one of his hands being lifted by a pair of wings, the other burdened by a sizeable royal orb depicting an ornately clad maiden. As per the Latin inscription, the figure illustrates the rift between the power of genius and costly pleasures.[49]

Bolswert redesigned van der Heyden's version, using the latter's idea of the weight in the form of a cross-bearing orb (a symbol of royal authority). Bolswert first used this solution in an engraving developed for Sucquet's 1620 volume, where a man with a leg attached to a royal orb was to depict a Christian desiring to follow Christ and at the same time overwhelmed by the weight of the world and his own sinful nature.[50]

On the other hand, the use of the same concept in the 1624 collection in accordance with Hugo's instructions is indicated by the scene taking place in the background of the print, which shows a boy with a tethered bird. This motif, inspired by a simile cited in a commentary from Pseudo-Chrysostom's *Sermo de paenitentia* (Sermon on penance), has its counterpart in Hugo's elegy. Thus, for the sake of formational purposes, a humanistic presentation was accorded a spiritual interpretation. It serves to illustrate the rift between longing for a heavenly homeland and an attachment to earthly matters, legitimized by a passage from the writings of the golden-mouthed doctor of the church (i.e., John Chrysostom [c.347–407]). This example not only shows that

---

47   Andrea Alciato, *Emblematum libellus* (Paris: Chrestien Wechel, 1534), 19.

48   See, e.g., the *alba amicorum* by Aernout van Buchell's (1565–1641), written between 1584 and 1614 (manuscript at the Kunstbibliothek Staatliche Museen zu Berlin, call no. Lipp oz 3, fol. 74ᵛ); Hans Ludwig Pfinzing von Henfenfeld (1570–1632), written between 1580 and 1625 (manuscript at the Staatsbibliothek Bamberg, call no. Msc. Hist.176, fol. 36ᵛ); or Burchard Grossman the Younger (1605–45) (manuscript at the Koninklijke Bibliotheek in The Hague, call no. 133 C 14, p. 183—entry dated March 24, 1631).

49   Jacob van der Heyden, *Pugillus facetiarum iconographicarum in studiosorum potissimum gratiam* (Strasburg, 1618), 12.

50   Antoine Sucquet, *Via vitae aeternae* (Antwerp: Typis Martini Nutii, 1620), illustration after 384. Shortly thereafter, the motif of the royal orb as a symbol of the temporal world would be comprehensively developed in the engravings of the emblem book *Typus mundi, in quo eius calamitates et pericula nec non Divini humanique Amoris antipathia emblematice proponuntur*, published in 1627.

the *Pia desideria* engravings boldly repurposed the resources of the emblem book genre for spiritual use but also demonstrates the rigorous imaginative collaboration between the printmaker and the volume's author.

It is worth mentioning that the Latin editions of Hugo's collection were essentially accompanied by two different sets of illustrations. The first consisted of Bolswert's original copperplate engravings (and their copies). The second set of engravings first appeared in a reprint published in late 1628 by Hendrick van Haestens's (c.1566–1629) printing house in Leuven (J.633; the censor's approval bears the date November 9 of that year). The new illustrations differed from the original ones not only in terms of artistic quality but also because of a number of compositional changes. Most of the scenes—originally portrayed indoors—take place outdoors (e.g., I, 4, 5, 10, II, 3, 6); some of the scenes likewise appear to have changed (e.g., the Soul lost in the labyrinth in emblem II, 2 has been placed on the earth globe; the Soul in front of the veil concealing the Bridegroom in engraving III, 12 is seen standing under the open sky). Also modified are the ties between the respective characters (e.g., I, 5); on top of that, in several engravings where the Soul originally appeared alone, depictions of the Divine Love were added, along with the new role he had been assigned (I, 9, 14, 15, III, 7).

Changes also affected the frontispiece. The central motif of the new frontispiece—modeled on the eponymous engraving of Wierix's *Cor Iesu amanti sacrum* series—is a monstrous-sized blazing heart; however, in this case, it is lifted toward God not by wings but by the personification of the soul kneeling under its weight. The personification of the Divine Love sets the heart on fire and guards its flame. The plurality of biblical authors and the concordant chorus of their sighs give way to the main characters of the collection, and the accompanying emphasis on the ardent bond that unites them. Since Haestens's edition saw a number of reprints across various outlets, it was also this set of engravings that soon became a template for numerous copies, which took modifications of the depicted scenes even further.

2.1.4   Emblem Composition: Elegies
The essential part of Hugo's book consists of poetic subscriptions (i.e., textual components of emblems, elaborating on images). These lengthy texts (some spanning over one hundred verses), written in the elegiac couplet, refer to the Neo-Latin tradition of the genre, and indirectly also to the oeuvre of poets of the Augustan era, most notably Ovid. The Jesuit author invoked this tradition directly, quoting a passage from *Ars amatoria* (The art of love; II, vv. 517–19) in one of his own elegies (III, 3, vv. 27–29). Just as the Polish Jesuit Maciej Kazimierz Sarbiewski (1595–1640) made a name for himself in Europe at the time with his Christianized version of Horatian songs, Hugo applied the style developed by the Roman elegiacs, repurposing it for his Christian poetry.

In these works, in accordance with the post-Tridentine custom of imitation, examples from ancient mythology and history were seamlessly combined with biblical characters, and both were often referenced through scholarly periphrases that appealed to the reader's erudition. Hugo's classicizing elegies were addressed to audiences proficient in the humanistic tradition—which was part of school curricula at the time—and well-versed in the Scriptures.

The young Anglican cleric Edmund Arwaker the Elder, who published a translation of *Pia desideria or Divine Addresses* in 1686, resented this confusion of biblical and pagan matter. In his preface, Arwaker made it clear that Hugo sometimes took his ancient erudition too far, which detracted from the religious tenor of his works.[51] Conversely, the lay translators who rendered Hugo's elegies into Polish were not offended by his syncretism. On the contrary, they seemed distinctly pleased with the opportunity to combine the humanistic education they had acquired in their youth with devotional reading. But when the subscriptions of emblem III, 6 were translated by a clerical person, the couplet that contained a comparison to the mythical Hercules (vv. 43–44) was omitted. The problem resurfaced when a free translation of the elegy was undertaken in the nineteenth century by Rev. Bonifacy Ostrzykowski (1800–74). Although Ostrzykowski praised Hugo's poetic talent beyond measure, equating him with the likes of Horace (65–8 BCE), William Shakespeare (1564–1616), and Johann Wolfgang von Goethe (1749–1832), he wrote of his verses that "strong are Hugo's thoughts, it is only the excess of mythological fables that obscures them," which is why he chose to leave out some of the examples derived from pagan antiquity.[52]

Despite what has been written on the subject,[53] the way Hugo's elegies follow the rules of meditation, dissected into successive points, is rather superficial. It is enough to compare emblem III, 12, whose engraving shows the Soul separated from the Divine Love by a veil, as the elegy expresses the longing to see the Bridegroom face to face, with the meditation of the Jesuit Kasper Drużbicki (1590–1662), also penned in 1624, which used an identical *compositio loci*

---

51   Herman Hugo, *Pia desideria or Divine Addresses in Three Books*, englished by Edm[und] Arwaker (London: Henry Bonwicke, 1686 [J.689]), fol. A5ʳ.

52   Hugo, *Pobożne pragnienia*, vi–vii.

53   See, e.g., Polman et al., "De Pia desideria va pater Herman Hugo s.j.," 36–37; Karl Josef Höltgen, "Emblem and Meditation: Some English Emblem Books and Their Jesuit Models," *Explorations in Renaissance Culture* 18 (1992): 58–66; Gabriele Rödter, "*Ordo naturalis* und meditative Struktur: Devotionslyrik im Kräftespiel von Emblematik, Rhetorik und Meditationspraxis dargelegt am Beispiel ausgewählter Kapitel der *Pia desideria* des Hermann Hugo s.j.," in *Religion und Religiosität im Zeitalter des Barock*, in Verbindung mit Barbara Becker-Cantarino, Heinz Schilling, Walter Sparn, ed. Dieter Breuer (Wiesbaden: Harrassowitz, 1995), 2:523–38.

(the composition of place; i.e., imagining the place in the meditation process in Ignatius of Loyola's *Spiritual Exercises*) as its starting point—"Imagine
yourself next to a veil, behind which stands the hidden Lord Jesus"[54]—to notice
some fundamental differences. Even if the closing verses of Hugo's poetic subscriptions were often subordinated to acts of the will, the elegies are a far cry
from the point-by-point sequential meditation promoted by the Jesuits. The
elegies were intended to captivate the reader primarily through the power of
dramatic emotion conveyed in classicizing poetic speech, saturated with clear
references to ancient authors.

In his preface, Arwaker highlighted another important feature of the *Pia
desideria* elegies. Despite being a Jesuit himself, Hugo consistently avoided
denominationally sensitive topics in his poetry. While he did mention purga-
tory in elegy I, 14, dedicated to four last things, and made a reference to the
sacrament of the Eucharist in subscription III, 12, which speaks of the desire to
experience God face to face, the volume is otherwise devoid of clear indications
of Hugo's affiliation to the Catholic faith.[55] The poet's decision to elaborate the
subscriptions in this fashion bolstered the interdenominational dimension of
his successful collection. After all, its influence extended not only to Catholic
countries but also to Lutheran, Calvinist, and Anglican territories, eventually
reaching Orthodox Russia.

2.1.5   Emblem Composition: Quotations from Exegetical Writings
In addition to the introductory emblem, each of the other forty-five works
in the collection is provided with an extensive set of quotations. In place of
the erudite scholia from the emblem books of Alciato, Joachim Camerarius the
Younger (1534–98), or Floris van Schoonhoven (1594–1648), which gained the
status of a summation of humanistic knowledge,[56] Hugo included an anthology of Bible verses and excerpts from the works of the doctors of the church,
as well as medieval and contemporary theologians. The volume of quotations
and their number varies. Typically, each elegy is followed by a dozen quotations
that span an average of five pages. Most of the excerpts come from the works
of St. Augustine (primarily from his commentaries on the book of Psalms) and
Pseudo-Augustine, mainly from *Liber meditationum* (Book of meditations) and

---

54   Kasper Drużbicki, "Rekolekcje sandomierskie," ed. Jan Maria Szymusiak, *Sacrum Poloniae
      Millennium* 11 (1965): 615–60, here 621.
55   Hugo, *Divine Addresses*, fol. A7ᵛ.
56   See, e.g., Daniel S. Russell, "Claude Mignault, Erasmus, and Simon Bouquet: The Function
      of the Commentaries on Alciato's Emblems," in *Mundus emblematicus*, 17–32; Karl A.E.
      Enenkel, "Florentius Schoonhovius *Emblemata partim moralia, partim etiam civilia*: Text
      and Paratext," in *Emblems of the Low Countries: A Book Historical Perspective*, ed. Alison
      Adams and Marleen van der Weij (Glasgow: Librairie Droz, 2003), 129–47.

Liber soliloquiorum animae ad Deum (The book of soul's soliloquies with God). Ranking second is St. Bernard of Clairvaux (including the most frequently cited commentaries on the Song of Songs), followed by St. Ambrose of Milan (*c.*340–97; Hugo readily drew on his explications of the psalms, especially *Expositio in Psalmum David CVIII* [The explanation of David's Psalm 108] and his treatise *De bono mortis* [On goodness of death]); fourth in line is St. Gregory the Great and his *Moralium libri sive Expositio in Librum beati Iob* (Books of morals, or the explanation on the book of the blessed Job).

The above ranking is not accidental. The quotations typically constitute an emotionally charged exegetical commentary on the verse selected as an inscription. Therefore, in the title of the collection Hugo referred to these excerpts as "the affections of the holy fathers." At the time, the writings of St. Augustine and the works of Pseudo-Augustine, whose works were attributed to the former, were very popular for their fervent style, among other things. When the Polish translation of the treatises attributed to St. Augustine was first published in 1617, the translator used the preface to laud the rhetorical texture of the works as the reason behind their success:

> For he wrote as he spoke. He spoke fervently and with frightening words, and wrote his books accordingly: he implored, rebuked, encouraged, bemoaned, weighed each problem thoroughly, oftentimes repeating his points in various ways, succumbing to passionate emotions, and spun a yarn about sin and hell, relentless in his choice of words and other ploys befitting an impassioned preacher, and hence his writing is not always smooth, as is usual in a fiery sermon. And with this admirable use of words, he compelled minds and held them captive to Christ.[57]

St. Augustine's attribute is a blazing heart; hence, it is no coincidence that it forms the background of the *Pia desideria* frontispiece in both of its most common graphic designs. St. Augustine's riveting style, dense with rhetorical figures, made him the foremost patristic patron of the affective tone employed in Hugo's poems.[58]

---

57 Aureliusz Augustyn, *Ksiąg pięcioro*, trans. [Jan Aland] (Vilnius: Akademia Jezuicka, 1617), fol. 6ʳ.

58 For the same reasons, St. Augustine also became the patron of Michel Hoyer's (1593–1650) 1629 emblem book *Flammulae amoris S.P. Augustini* (see Arnoud Visser, "Commonplaces of Catholic Love: Otto van Veen, Michel Hoyer, and St Augustine between Humanism and the Counter-Reformation," in *Learned Love*, ed. Els Stronks and Peter Boot, assisted by Dagmar Stiebral [The Hague: DANS, 2007], 33–48; Feike Dietz, "Under the Cover of Augustine: Augustinian Spirituality and Catholic Emblems in the Seventeenth-Century

The excerpts were meant to demonstrate that not a single elegy in the collection depicts a randomly arranged scene between the Divine Love and the Soul but instead represents a symbolic visualization supported by the centuries-old teachings of the church. For example, the engraving to the emblem I, 5, showing the Divine Love fashioning human vessels at the potter's wheel, refers to the biblical image of God as a potter (Jer. 18:2–6), recalled in the accompanying excerpts along with the relevant interpretation of medieval theologians: Rupert of Deutz (c.1075–1130; *De Trinitate et operibus eius* [On the Trinity and its works] 2,20–1 and *In Hieremiam prophetam commentariorum liber* [Book of commentaries on Prophet Jeremiah] 10,18), Hugh of Saint-Cher (c.1200–63; *Liber Ieremiae* [Book of Jeremiah] 18), and Pseudo-Augustine (*Liber soliloquiorum animae ad Deum* 20,2 and 31,7).

The anthology of exegetical excerpts was attached to cater to readers with theological interests, primarily monks and clergymen. The printers quickly realized that this might not be as relevant to some lay audiences. Just four years after the original edition, the Leuven publisher van Haestens compiled a reprint in which the patristic excerpts were reduced to a single- or two-sentenced quotation (it was also the very edition in which Bolswert's engravings were replaced by their redactions). Once Hugo demonstrated that the artistic solutions he proposed were grounded in the subject literature, the complex theological apparatus became superfluous for non-specialist readers. It was all the easier to dispose of it, and thus render the volume considerably slimmer (by a total of nearly 250 pages), thereby significantly reducing the cost of printing and increasing the profit on each copy sold.[59] It was precisely for this reason that the idea caught on with other printers. The edition with a simplified theological commentary was adopted by the Antwerp publishing house of Hendrik Aertssens the Elder (1586–1658), which also published editions with a full theological apparatus, and from then on Hugo's volume was reissued in both versions simultaneously.

Reception-wise, the decision to trim the collection's volume proved to be an apt one. Of the dozens of national adaptations produced throughout the seventeenth and the first half of the eighteenth centuries, few were tempted to translate the complete set of excerpts, as they were not that relevant for lay

---

Dutch Republic," in *Augustine beyond the Book: Intermediality, Transmediality, and Reception*, ed. Karla Pollmann and Meredith J. Gill [Leiden: Brill, 2012], 167–94).

59   Not all readers welcomed this innovation. One copy of this edition that I encountered was interfoliated using blank pages on which the owner had transcribed Hugo's exegetical commentary from the complete edition (copy from the University of Wrocław Library, call no. 319203).

readers. Instead, the exegetical excerpts played a key role in vernacular adaptations of Hugo's collection intended for monastic readership.

2.1.6   Structure of the Collection

Also significant among the solutions adopted by Hugo was the division of the emblems into three books. After the introductory work, which was left unnumbered, the author divided the remaining forty-five into three parts of fifteen emblems each. The titles of the successive books refer to the division of spiritual development into stages of purification (*via purgativa*), enlightenment (*via illuminativa*), and union (*via unitiva*), as codified in the Western spiritual tradition by St. Bonaventure's (1221–74) treatise *De triplici via* (On the triple path). This division helped popularize the model of meditation proposed in Loyola's *Spiritual Exercises*, where, of the four weeks of exercises, the first was subordinated to purification, the second and third to enlightenment, and the fourth to the union of the retreatant's soul with God, respectively. By the end of the first quarter of the seventeenth century, this stratification had spread through numerous studies promoting meditation as the most effective type of mental prayer. It was also employed in meditative books supplemented with emblematic engravings. In the 1620 volume *Via vitae aeternae* by Sucquet, Hugo's superior at the Brussels Jesuit college, the chapters were organized into the following books: "Via incipientium" (The way of beginners), "Via proficientium" (The way of the proficient), and "Via perfectorum" (The way of the perfect).[60]

Hugo altered this division significantly, substituting theological terminology for titles with distinctly emotional overtones: *Gemitus Animae poenitentis* (Groans of the penitent soul), *Vota Animae sanctae* (Desires of the holy soul), and *Suspiria Animae amantis* (Sighs of the loving soul), which corresponded with other measures that subordinated the collection to dramatic affections.

The censor's approval attached to the first edition, dated November 11, 1623, betrays the original intent behind the print's title, which was to include information on the division of the volume into three books: "Pia desideria, gemitus et suspiria Animae christianae, elegiis, emblematis et s[anctum] patrum scriptis illustrata" (Pious desires, groans, and sighs of the Christian soul, illustrated

---

60   See, e.g., Gabriele D. Rödter, *Via piae animae: Grundlagenuntersuchung zur emblematischen Verknüpfung von Bild und Wort in den* Pia desideria *(1624) des Herman Hugo s.j. (1588–1629)* (Frankfurt am Main: Peter Lang, 1992), 27–28; Black, "Popular Devotional Emblematics," 3–8. However, the assignment of the emblems to the three stages of spiritual development in Hugo's collection did not have to be modeled on Sucquet's volume, since such a division was widely used in various types of contemplative prayer.

with elegies, emblems, and writings of the holy fathers).[61] Such a notation suggests that the eponymous formula of "pia desideria" was originally meant to refer exclusively to the first book of the collection, divided into sections devoted to desires, moans, and sighs. It also indicates that, originally, the lyrical heroine was not accompanied by epithets indicating her progression en route to the mystical union. Their addition in the printed version emphasized the successive nature of the meditative path as presented in Hugo's book.

When *Pia desideria* was published, the book market was not short of collections of spiritual exercises, illustrated with engravings that were perfect aids visualizing the scene constituting the subject of a given meditation. One example of this trend was the volume by French Jesuits Étienne Luzvic (1567–1640) and Étienne Binet (1569–1639), whose 1627 Latin translation of *Cor Deo devotum, Iesu pacifici Salomonis thronus regius* (Heart dedicated to God, Solomon's royal throne of the peaceful Jesus) followed each image, modeled on an engraving of the *Cor Iesu amanti sacrum* cycle, with a preamble and a point-by-point breakdown of the meditation with an introductory prayer, acts of prayer, and a recommendation to recite the *Pater noster* and *Ave Maria* prayers at the end of the exercise. Hugo proposed a volume of a different nature: the mode of meditation was written into his elegies in a decidedly more discreet manner. Instead of a list of successive stages of a spiritual exercise, he opted for a message that relied on strong emotions grounded in meticulously selected biblical verses and passages from exegetical literature, as well as erudite elegies and adequately composed engravings. Developed according to this formula, Hugo's emblem book turned into a pan-European bestseller.

2.2   The Popularity of Pia desideria *in the Polish–Lithuanian Commonwealth*

As in the rest of Europe, emblem books—especially those with religious themes—were very popular in the Polish–Lithuanian Commonwealth. Popularity-wise, *Pia desideria* clearly stands out against this backdrop.

The presence of a title in ancient book collections can be studied in two ways: by determining the owners of preserved copies on the basis of the surviving provenance notes, and by analyzing book inventories, which in the case of private individuals were usually compiled in connection with inheritance-related matters, and in the case of religious libraries for record-keeping purposes. Both methods are not faultless (not every owner of a book signed it with their name; not everyone who signed it was a reader; inventories of movables account first of all for valuable books, e.g., those with expensive bindings, while unframed

---

61   Herman Hugo, *Pia desideria* (Antwerp: Hendrik Aertssens, 1624 [J.628/N.345]), 414.

ones were sometimes omitted, etc.) and provide highly selective data on the actual reception of a specific title (the number of surviving copies is but a fraction of those kept in seventeenth- and eighteenth-century collections; moreover, the available inventories account for a mere sliver of the actual number of inventories compiled at the time). However, when studied together, they offer a glimpse of the reading trends and social groups particularly interested in a given title. Therefore, it is worthwhile at this point to recount a reconnaissance concerning the presence of Hugo's collection in Polish and Lithuanian book collections and outline the resulting conclusions about the nature of its reception.[62]

2.2.1   Male Readers

Most Latin editions of *Pia desideria* have been preserved in the book collections of monasteries and monastic schools. Two copies of the first edition were in the possession of the library of the Discalced Carmelites in Nowy Wiśnicz. They belonged to a collection of more than three hundred volumes donated in 1630 by Stanisław Lubomirski (1583–1649), whose sons had purchased them in Leuven or Cologne during an educational voyage.[63] The collection of the Jesuit novitiate in Vilnius was host to a copy of the 1628 edition (J.631/N.346 or J.632);[64] a Latin edition dated 1629 (J.635) found its way into the book collection of the Augustinian monastery at St. Catherine's Church in Kraków;[65] in turn, a copy of the 1632 edition (J.636/N.347) was owned by the Jesuit college at St. Peter and Paul's Church in Kraków[66] and the Carthusian monastery in Gidle near Radomsko.[67] The monastery in Gidle was a branch convent of the monastery in Kartuzy, whose library once contained two copies of *Pia desideria*

---

62   Radosław Grześkowiak, "Polska recepcja *Pia desideria*: Typy odbioru religijnych zbiorów emblematycznych," in *Dialogi dzieł dawnych: Studia o intertekstualności literatury staropolskiej* (Gdańsk: Wydawnictwo UG, 2018), 169–218, here 176–77, 181–82, 192–93.

63   Józef Długosz, "Biblioteka klasztoru karmelitów bosych w Wiśniczu (1630–1649)," *Archiwa, biblioteki i muzea kościelne* 13 (1966): 91–169, here 152, 114.

64   See *Catalogus librorum Bibliothecae Novitiatus Vilnensis Societatis Jesu confectus Anno Domini 1748*, manuscript kept by the University of Vilnius, call no. F.1–C 47, 155. Page 7 contains an item that reads, "*Pia desideria* P[atris] Hugonis, Vilnae, Anno 1722," which presumably refers to the manuscript version, since the edition published that year, much less the one printed in Vilnius, remains unknown (information courtesy of Prof. Magdalena Górska).

65   Copy from the Jagiellonian Library in Kraków, call no. Aug. 5460.

66   Copy from the Jagiellonian Library in Kraków, call no. Teol. 2290.

67   Copy from the Library of the Metropolitan Seminary of the Archdiocese of Warsaw, call no. O.50.59 (75639).

whose date of publication is unknown.[68] The Piarist college in Warsaw owned a copy of the 1676 edition (J.654/N.354),[69] while a copy of the 1682 edition (J.657) was kept at the Bernardine monastery in Tykocin.[70] The library of the Warsaw Missionary House at the Church of the Holy Cross held at least three different editions of the Latin print, published in 1645 (J.641/N.349), 1673 (J.653), and 1682 (J.657), respectively.[71] The well-known educational reformer of the Enlightenment era, Piarist Stanislaw Konarski (1700–73), donated a copy of the 1721 Cologne edition (J.669) to the Collegium Nobilium, a college he had founded in Warsaw.[72]

Second in terms of the number of copies owned were clergymen and consecrated readers of the volume. One of the owners of the Milan edition of 1634 (J.637) was the Franciscan friar Benedykt Michniewicz (dates unknown);[73] a copy of another edition, dated 1659 (J.649/N.351), bears the signature of an unknown Warsaw canon;[74] yet another issue, dated 1657 (J.648/N.350), was signed in 1766 by the Discalced Augustinian Dominik of St. Ferdinand.[75] Also surviving are a number of volumes that were passed down between several generations of clerical readers: for example, a copy of the 1628 edition (J.631/N.346) was signed by the Basilian Hilarion Kuczerewicz and two Jesuit priests, Mikołaj Trzebiński (1690–c.1773) and Jerzy Komparzewicz.[76] An unknown edition was used by the parish priest of Firlejowo and subsequent canon of Kyiv, Benedykt Chmielowski (1700–63), who quoted Hugo's couplet (II, 1, vv. 45–46) in his compilation-type encyclopedia *Nowe Ateny* (New Athens), clarifying that it represented a spiritual version of van Veen's emblem that bore an analogous message (*Amorum emblemata* 2).[77]

---

68   They were listed in an inventory dated 1770. See Krzysztof Nierzwicki, *Biblioteki kartuzji kaszubskiej oraz jej konwentów filialnych w Berezie Kartuskiej i Gidlach* (Pelplin: Bernardinum, 2001), 417 (nos. 1331 and 1332).

69   *Catalogus librorum Bibliothecae Collegii Regii Varsaviensis Clericorum Regularium Scholarum Piarum factus anno Domini 1796*, [n.p.], 60.

70   Copy from the Library of the Metropolitan Seminary of the Archdiocese of Białystok, call no. S-639.

71   Copies from the Library of the Metropolitan Seminary of the Archdiocese of Warsaw, call nos. O.93.21 (77646); F.64.21 (67671); R.21.43 (64473).

72   Copy from the Library of the Metropolitan Seminary of the Archdiocese of Warsaw, call no. B.III.42a (58493).

73   Copy from the Jagiellonian Library in Kraków, call no. Teol. 4802 I.

74   Copy from the University of Wrocław Library, call no. 474490.

75   Copy from the Pontifical Academy of Theology in Kraków, call no. XVII.2333.

76   Library of the Metropolitan Seminary of the Archdiocese of Białystok, call no. S-640.

77   Benedykt Chmielowski, *Nowe Ateny*, 2nd ed. (Lviv: Kolegium Jezuickie, 1754), 1:part 1, 1176–77.

The popularity of Hugo's volume was not limited to the clergy. Copies of the collection were also purchased by lay readers, strongly diversified in terms of their social background. *Pia desideria* was read by magnates, such as the connoisseur of emblem literature and voivod of Kraków, Aleksander Michał Lubomirski (1614–77), whose collection included such items as Heinsius's *Emblemata amatoria*, van Veen's *Amorum emblemata* and *Emblemata Horatiana*, Sucquet's *Via vitae aeternae*, van Haeften's *Schola cordis*, as well as volumes by Camerarius, Jacobus Typotius (1540–1601), Diego de Saavedra Fajardo (1584–1648), and Julius Wilhelm Zincgref (1591–1635),[78] voivod of Volhynia, Jan Franciszek Stadnicki (1656–1713),[79] and the translators of the collection's elegies, namely the voivod of Minsk, Jan Kazimierz Żaba, and the court marshal of Lithuania, Aleksander Teodor Lacki. The book was also present in the libraries of aristocratic palaces. Two owners of the volume, the standard-bearer of Przemyśl, Krzysztof Tomasz Drohojowski (*c*.1630–89), and poet Jakub Teodor Trembecki (1643–*c*.1719), will be discussed below. A copy of one of the eighteenth-century editions was signed by the chamberlain of the Ruthenian voivodship, the geometer and builder Stanisław Mikoszewski (dates unknown), noted for his fondness for Jesuit literature.[80] Copies of Hugo's volume were also purchased by the affluent bourgeoisie, such as Ludwik Walerian Alembek (d.1704), a Lviv physician and owner of a lavish book collection.[81]

Those who could not afford an illustrated import print could always transcribe it themselves. One such transcript of the 1645 edition of *Pia desideria* (J.641/N.349)—which includes the full text of the edition, along with the publisher's address and an acronym of the printer's privilege—was made by an anonymous Polish reader.[82]

This enumeration points to a fundamental stratification among Polish–Lithuanian readers: the volume's religious nature, supplied with exegetical excerpts, appealed primarily to a clerical audience, while its emotional character, attractive engravings, and erudite elegies also made it a favorite among readers unaffiliated with the church institutions.

---

78   Józef Długosz, "Księgozbiór Aleksandra Michała Lubomirskiego w świetle inwentarza z 1678 r.," *Ze skarbca kultury* 23 (1972): 7–52, here 32–38.

79   See *Index librorum conscriptus in arcae Lesce die 18 octobris 1697-mo*, manuscript kept by the Library of the Ossoliński National Institute in Wrocław, call no. 3927/III.

80   Copy from the Jagiellonian Library in Kraków, call no. Teol. 4802 I, 17. An identical provenance note ("Ex libris Stanislai Mikoszewski") can be found in three early eighteenth-century prints by the Jesuit theologian Georg Gengell (1657–1727), kept by the Vernadsky National Library of Ukraine in Kyiv.

81   Edward Różycki, "Inwentarz książek lwowianina Ludwika Waleriana Alembeka z 1704 roku," *Roczniki biblioteczne* 40, nos. 1/2 (1996): 109–38, here 115.

82   Copy from the University of Łódź Library, call no. Akc. 6984.

Another division of the volume's audience concerns denominational issues. Although few testimonies of cross-confessional reception have survived from the territories of the Polish–Lithuanian state, the ones we know of take on special significance against the background of analogous trends in the neighboring countries, especially in Lutheran Silesia or the Duchy of Pomerania. For it appears that *Pia desideria* met with keen interest among Protestants, especially among Calvinists and Polish Brethren (also known as Arians or Unitarians).

In the aforementioned copy of the 1634 Milan edition, which was later owned by the Franciscan Michniewicz and the chamberlain Mikoszewski, the former added Polish translations of biblical inscriptions in several emblems (I, 1, vv. 3–7). Most interesting among them is the addition made to the Bible verse quoted in emblem I, 3, which, unlike in the Vulgate, does feature God's name: "Have mercy on me, Jehovah, for I am faint; heal me, Jehovah, for my bones are in agony" (Ps. 6:2). The Polish verses were taken from a 1572 Arian translation of the Bible by Szymon Budny (*c.*1530–93). Given its strong denominational profiling, the audience of Budny's version was limited to the Polish Brethren. Thus, its use is indicative of the reader's affiliation with a specific religious denomination.

The 1676 inventory of books owned by Drohojowski, who belonged to a well-known family of protectors of Calvinism, lists two widely read titles by Jesuit authors, mentioned amid religious works penned by various luminaries of the Reformation. In addition to the Latin–Polish edition of *Somnium vitae humanae* (Human life's dream) by the German Jesuit Jakob Balde (1604–68), translated into Polish by the Jesuit Zygmunt Brudecki (1610–47), Drohojowski's inventory included a volume labeled as: "*Pia desideria* Hugonis Soc[ietatis] Iesu cum iconibus" (*Pia desideria* by Hugo of the Society of Jesus, with pictures).[83]

The poet Jakub Teodor Trembecki, who also collected poems by his contemporaries (including the Calvinist Daniel Naborowski [1573–1640], the Arian Zbigniew Morsztyn, and the early works of the Arian period of Wacław Potocki [1621–96]), was a son of an Arian minister. However, he was not drawn to his father's faith: while remaining in the service of the Calvinist Radziwiłł family, he converted to Calvinism, and while serving the Catholic families of Słuszka and Denhoff, he changed his denomination to Catholicism. A copy of the Antwerp edition of *Pia desideria* from 1659 has survived (J.649/N.351), which Trembecki purchased in 1676 for the price of three florins and ten cents.

---

83   Kamila Schuster, "O autorstwie *Regestru ksiąg* z roku 1676 i ich właścicielu Krzysztofie Tomaszu Drohojowskim," *Ze skarbca kultury* 29 (1977): 43–61, here 60; Maria Barłowska, "Litteraria w rękopiśmiennym inwentarzu ksiąg Krzysztofa Tomasza Drohojowskiego," *Rocznik przemyski* 48, no. 2 (2012): 273–84, here 282.

One person who abided by the faith of the Polish Brethren was Trembecki's peer Zbigniew Morsztyn, author of an adaptation of *Pia desideria*. And although his version was based on a compilation by a certain Capuchin friar, Morsztyn was also familiar with the original edition of the collection by the Jesuit Hugo.

2.2.2 Women Readers

The examples enumerated above show a tendency in the reception of *Pia desideria* to blur the distinctions between the clergy, consecrated, and laypeople on the one hand, and Catholics and representatives of Reformed denominations on the other. It is no coincidence that the listed owners and readers of the volume were men (this also applies to institutional libraries). Hugo's collection was written in Latin, and it owed its international career to this linguistic medium, which rendered it accessible to any European who took a relevant course in school. However, the same medium precluded women—whose education only exceptionally included studies in Latin—from joining the ranks of those who relished in Hugo's volume. The creators of erotic collections of the likes of Heinsius's *Emblemata amatoria* were well aware of that; in fact, in a poem addressed to Dutch maidens, Heinsius states that it was Venus who told him to teach Cupid the Dutch language.[84] Most volumes of love emblems were supplied with sets of subscriptions written in several vernacular languages, which rendered them equally accessible to women readers.

The religious subject matter of *Pia desideria* and the erotic manner of its elaboration were perfectly aligned with the feminine horizon of expectations. It was only the language of the original collection that prevented the book from being enjoyed by women readers. The desire to expand the target audience to include women was the main driver behind the extensive international vernacularization campaign for Hugo's emblem book.

The many adapters of Hugo's work into national languages were guided by the motivation best expressed by Anglican clergyman Edmund Arwaker the Elder in his preface to the 1686 translation of *Pia desideria or Divine Addresses*:

> From my first acquaintance with this Author, which was as early as I was able to understand him, I found him so pleasing and agreeable, that I wish'd he were taught to speak English, that those who cou'd not understand him in his own language might by that means partake of the satisfaction and advantage I, at least, receiv'd in my conversation with

---

84   [Daniël Heinsius], *Aen de joncvrouwen van Hollandt*, verses 17–22, in *Emblemata amatoria: Iam demum emendata* (Amsterdam: Dirck Pieterszoon, 1608), fol. A2ᵛ.

him. And finding that not any pen had been employ'd about the Work
[...], and such an exellent piece of Devotion be lost to those who wou'd
prise it most, the Religious Ladies of our Age, I resolv'd to engage in the
attempt, and the rather, because the Subject was sutable to my Calling
as a Clergyman, as the Sense was to my Fancy, as an humble Admirer of
Poetry, especially such as is Divine.[85]

Prior to Arwaker, Lacki had made an identical case for undertaking a translation of Hugo into Polish. In the draft of the 1671 preface, which eventually
did not appear in print, one may learn that Hugo depicted the ardent love of
the Soul for the heavenly Bridegroom in captivating verse. But since he did so
in Latin, the Soul could not appeal to the women of the Polish–Lithuanian
state, and therefore Lacki resolved to "teach it" the Polish language.[86] The
pious desires verbalized by Lacki and Arwaker, common to the international
host of translators and adaptors of Hugo's collection, were answered, and their
projected female reception of the work became a reality, including in the
Polish–Lithuanian state.

The surviving copies of the Latin original in Poland have no notes indicating that their owner/reader was a woman. The case is different with the Polish
translations. One of the copies of the first edition of Lacki's 1673 translation
bears the signature of its owner, one "Mrs. Przyborowska."[87] Another copy
of this edition was owned by the Bydgoszcz municipal judge Jan Kazimierz
Grabski (d.1723), who made an entry in the inventory of his book collection,
stating that he had lent the volume to his wife.[88] The rich collection of the
Discalced Carmelite Nuns in Wesoła Street in Kraków contains no copies of the
Latin edition of *Pia desideria*; at the same time, it holds as many as three copies
of Lacki's translation.[89] This translation was also part of the collections of the
Visitandine Convent in Kraków and the Benedictine Convent in Sandomierz.[90]

---

85   Hugo, *Divine Addresses*, fol. A2ʳ.
86   Radosław Grześkowiak, "'Zwyczajem kawalerów ziemskich postępuje z nią Oblubieniec':
      Pierwotna dedykacja *Pobożnych pragnień* Aleksandra Teodora Lackiego jako autorski pro-
      jekt lektury emblematów Hermana Hugona," *Pamiętnik literacki* 106, no. 1 (2015): 199–227,
      here 222.
87   Copy from the University of Warsaw Library, file no. Sd.713.2496, fol. A1ʳ.
88   Paulina Buchwald-Pelcowa, "Inwentarz biblioteki Jana Kazimierza Grabskiego z 1691
      roku," in Buchwald-Pelcowa, *Historia literatury i historia książki: Studia nad książką i
      literaturą od średniowiecza po wiek XVIII* (Kraków: Universitas, 2005), 341–58, here 353.
89   Copies from the Library of the Convent of the Discalced Carmelite Nuns in Wesoła Street,
      Kraków, file nos. 136/1, 418/1, 1665/1 (they were copies of the 1697 edition).
90   Copies from the National Museum in Kraków, file no. VIII–XVII.1563; and the Diocesan
      Library in Sandomierz, file no. 25653.

Once the French language came into vogue, a combined adaptation of Hugo's and van Veen's devotional collections in the form of the 1717 volume *L'âme amante de son Dieu* (The soul loving its God; J.694) found its way to Polish and Lithuanian readers and was read by the likes of the magnate Anna Radziwiłł née Sanguszko (1676–1746), who owned a copy of the book herself.[91]

In anticipation of more detailed considerations, one should state that Polish adaptations of *Pia desideria* were developed for women and were sought after by female readers. Thus, perhaps the most important barrier to the reception of this book was broken. Hugo's *Pia desideria* proved to be an extremely attractive guide to communion with God for people of different social status, religion, and gender.

3 Adaptations of *Pia desideria* Based on Its Engravings

3.1 *The Role of Devotional Engravings in Propagating Personal Piety*
Early engravings on religious themes in the form of book illustrations or loose prints had a strong impact on the public, serving as a useful catechetical tool. In order to understand the importance of engravings to spiritual development, it suffices to look into the seventeenth- and eighteenth-century biographies written by Discalced Carmelite nuns to uplift their fellow sisters. According to the biography of one of the most prominent Polish Daughters of Carmel, Teresa Barbara of the Blessed Sacrament (Teofila Zadzikowa née Kretkowska [1609–70]), the genesis of her interest in monastic life began with an engraving she had received as a gift. As a nun, Zadzikowa avidly collected devotional engravings, which strongly facilitated her spiritual development. Even when sensing her impending death, she would ask for an engraving presenting the deposition of Jesus from the cross to be placed before her eyes, so that, as she lay dying, she could focus her thoughts on what was crucial at the time of her transition to a better world.[92]

Zadzikowa's biography included an interesting testimony to the reception of emblematic engravings. When the Discalced Carmelite nuns at St. Joseph's Convent in Lublin perused van Haeften's *Regia via crucis* (Royal way of the cross), they were not so much taken by the Latin text, incomprehensible

---

91   Wanda Karkucińska, *Anna z Sanguszków Radziwiłłowa (1676–1746): Działalność gospodarcza i mecenat* (Warsaw: Neriton, 2000), 264.

92   Czesław Gil, ed., *Żywot matki Barbary od Najśw[iętszego] Sakramentu (Zadzikowej), karmelitanki bosej (1609–1670)* (Kraków: Wydawnictwo Karmelitów Bosych, 2013), 35, 154, 186, 239, 263.

to most of them, as they were by the copper engravings of Cornelis Galle I (1576–1650). The nuns took an avid interest in the illustration in chapter I, 3, depicting fourteen crosses symbolizing different forms of mortification. Of these, the nuns would choose a cross that represented the type of suffering they wished to subject themselves to in their ascetic practices. These choices were accompanied by extreme feelings, which ranged from fear and disgust to euphoric joy.[93]

These accounts demonstrate that the meditative reception of devotional engravings was capable of generating strong, even corporeal reactions. They also prove that, in the case of Latin emblem books, the incomprehensible text did not altogether preclude them from attracting the attention of women readers. The latter focused on the engravings, whose iconography was so familiar that they could easily manage to decipher even complex allegorical meanings. Whether in the form of a book illustration or a loose print, both inside and outside the cloister walls, engravings with religious themes were a source of profound experience and spiritual edification.

3.2   Two Adaptations Dedicated to Princess Katarzyna Radziwiłł née Sobieska

3.2.1   Religiosity and Emblematic Interests of the Princess

The most important promoter of Western religious emblem books in the Polish–Lithuanian Commonwealth was not any ecclesiastical dignitary or Jesuit author but the younger sister of King Jan III Sobieski (1629–96, r.1674–96), Katarzyna (1634–94), wife of Prince Władysław Dominik Zasławski-Ostrogski (1618–56) from 1650 to 1656, and spouse of Prince Michał Kazimierz Radziwiłł (1635–80) between 1658 and 1680. Known for her affected religiosity, the magnate not only initiated numerous church foundations but also nurtured her own individual piety. Both in the parish church in Biała and across all her residences, the princess ordered separate cells to be adopted for ascetic practices and prayer meditations. One of them was recounted by the Jesuit Stanisław Bielicki (1656–1718). It was filled with hair shirts, bloodied whips, and iron cilices, blunted from frequent use. In addition to instruments intended to mortify the flesh, the cell was also equipped with pious books and devotional engravings pinned to the walls.[94]

---

93   *Żywot Zadzikowej*, 202–3. See Benedictus van Haeften, *Regia via crucis* (Antwerp: Officina Plantiniana, 1635), 16.

94   Stanisław Bielicki, *Matka publicznych żalów* [...], *Katarzyna z Sobieszyna Radziwiłłowa* [...], *pogrzebowym kazaniem opłakana* (Warsaw: Szkoła Pijarska, 1695), fol. K2ʳ. It should be noted that similar ascetic practices, consisting in the mortification of the flesh and

Although Katarzyna's tuition was limited to learning how to read and write in Polish, she developed the habit of diligently reading religious works at an early age. She would constantly read the lives of saints, collections of sermons, and exegetical writings. She was particularly interested in the books devoted to the passion of Christ, the most frequent subject of her meditations.[95]

Since the princess was unfamiliar with Latin, the aforementioned works were limited to Polish publications. With respect to Western European prints, her attention was drawn to illustrated emblem books. Although she did not understand their text, she analyzed the accompanying engravings, which were the sustenance for her devotional impressions, and commissioned literary adaptations of these works from the poets who were sponsored by her two husbands. Typically, these were not translations (the original texts, which were unintelligible to her, were of no interest) but rather adaptations in the form of poetic commentaries on the engravings, that is, the element of emblem books that the princess found the most attractive. This led to the creation of several Polish collections, two of which are of interest to us for their links to *Pia desideria*, namely *Nabożne westchnienia* (Devotional sighs) by the Jesuit Mieleszko (Meleszko, Maleszko [1607–67]) and a collection of emblems by Morsztyn, both mentioned above. Artistically, the two collections rank among the most interesting poetic emblem cycles of the Polish baroque. Therefore, it is all the more regrettable that the princess elected to enjoy them in solitude and was not interested in financing their publication. Hence, both collections have survived only as handwritten copies.

3.2.2   Mikołaj Mieleszko's Adaptation: *Nabożne westchnienia*
The Jesuit priest Mikołaj Mieleszko descended from a Ruthenian noble family.[96] For the purposes of the triennial Jesuit report, he most often identified himself as a Ruthenian ("Roxolanus," "Ruthenus"), and less often as a Podolian ("Podolanus") or Volhynian ("Volinensis"). At the age of twenty-one, he entered the novitiate at St. Stephen's Church in Kraków, whose rector at the time was the charismatic priest and eminent theological writer Kasper Drużbicki. Upon graduation, Mieleszko went on to study philosophy and theology. He then

---

senses (often to the detriment of one's health), were typical of the religiosity of Polish and Lithuanian women in the seventeenth century.

95   Radosław Grześkowiak and Jakub Niedźwiedź, *Wstęp*, in Mikołaj Mieleszko, *Emblematy*, ed. Radosław Grześkowiak and Jakub Niedźwiedź (Warsaw: Neriton, 2010), 60–61; Jarosław Pietrzak, *Księżna dobrodziejka: Katarzyna z Sobieskich Radziwiłłowa (1634–1694)* (Warsaw: Muzeum w Wilanowie, 2016), 64–66, 387–90.

96   Biographical data on the author was collected and compiled by Jakub Niedźwiedź: Grześkowiak and Niedźwiedź, *Wstęp*, 50–64.

served as a teacher of the humanities at colleges in Sandomierz, Lublin, Vinnytsia in Podolia (present-day Ukraine), Ostroh in Volhynia (present-day Ukraine), Brest (present-day Belarus), among others, and spent several years as a missionary, including in Turov (present-day Belarus) and Novhorod-Siverskyi (present-day Ukraine).

After the marriage of Prince Michał Kazimierz Radziwiłł to Katarzyna, née Sobieska, which took place in June 1658, Mieleszko was named court chaplain to the newly wedded couple. What helped him in this appointment was the literary gift he had presented the year before to the widow of Prince Władysław Dominik Zasławski-Ostrogski. It was a clean copy of two poetic cycles compiled to accompany engravings of popular emblematic collections, *Pia desideria* and the 1627 volume *Cor Deo devotum, Iesu pacifici Salomonis thronus regius* by the Jesuit Charles Musart (1582–1653). The title page of the first collection bears the date 1657, while the dedication to the second one identifies it as an Easter gift. The poet's contacts with the princess thus date back to at least March 1657, and probably lasted longer, since in the dedication to *Nabożne westchnienia* the author mentions her graciousness, which he had experienced on previous occasions. As a teacher of poetics, Mieleszko was well suited to this literary task, and his collections prove that, in addition to his technical skills, he did not lack poetic talent.

At least nineteen Latin editions of *Pia desideria* had been published before 1657, when the clean copy of *Nabożne westchnienia* was offered to the princess. Since Mieleszko's cycle was heavily linked to the engravings, it is not difficult to conclude that the poet used an edition supplied with the copperplate engravings by Bolswert (or faithful copies thereof). This excludes the editions devoid of illustrations (e.g., French editions of 1625 [J.629/F.333], 1635 [J.639], and 1648 [J.644]) and editions featuring a set of engravings modified in van Haestens's 1628 release (J.633); the latter included different iconographic elements that one would look for in vain in the Polish adaptation. The subscription devoted to the frontispiece refers to a copperplate attributed to Bolswert, which excludes editions featuring a different copperplate on the title page (e.g., the Cologne edition of 1635 [J.638]).

The phrases used by Mieleszko in the expanded title, *Nabożne westchnienia* [...] *od Hermana Hugona Societatis Iesu łacińskim wierszem, obrazami i naukami z doktorów ś[więtych] zebranemi wyrażone* (Devotional sighs, by the Jesuit Herman Hugo, expressed in Latin verse, engravings, and teachings collected from the holy doctors), are a translation of the original print titled: *Pia desideria emblematis, elegiis et affectibus s[anctorum] patrum illustrata authore Ermanno Hugo Societatis Iesu*; this, in turn, excludes the Latin editions whose title was shortened to *Pia desideria lib[ri] III* (editions of 1628 [J.632], 1629

[J.635], and 1632 [J.636/N.347]). Finally, Mieleszko's preface mentions the original dedication to Pope Urban VIII (1568–1644, r.1623–44), which was altered, for example, in the edition pressed in Graz in 1651 (J.645/G.362), dedicated to King Ferdinand IV Habsburg of Hungary (1633–54, r.1646–54).

Only three early editions meet all of the above criteria. These include the releases by the Antwerp printing house of Aertssens the Elder dated 1624 (J.628/N.345) and 1627 (J.630), and an edition by the Amsterdam printer Pieter Jacobszoon Paets (1587–after 1657), whose reprint appeared in 1628 (J.631/N.346; instead of the original copperplates, Paets used woodcut copies by Christoffel van Sichem the Younger [1581–1658]). A copy of one of those editions must have served as the basis for the adaptation of the future chaplain of the Radziwiłłs.

Mieleszko's adaptation is currently known in two versions preserved as handwritten copies. An anonymous copy of the earlier redaction (incomplete, as it breaks off at the third verse of subscription III, 15) is preserved in the book collection of the Benedictine nuns in Sandomierz.[97]

The Sandomierz convent was founded by the Benedictine nuns of the Chełmno reform, who stressed the role of intellectual formation in their spiritual life, along with devotional reading and practicing the Ignatian model of meditation. The first educational institution to have hired Mieleszko was the Jesuit college in Sandomierz (Collegium Gostomianum), where he worked as a grammar teacher in the 1633/34 school year. And since the pastoral guidance over the Sandomierz Benedictine nuns was exercised by the local Jesuits (including Mieleszko's teacher, Drużbicki), Mieleszko may have become acquainted with the nuns, which is what led him to share the text of his adaptation with them years later.

A copy of the original redaction is titled: *Nabożne westchnienie pragnącej Boga Duszy trojakiemu stanowi ludzi służące: do Boga nawracającym, od Boga oświeconym, z Bogiem złączonym, w których obrazy Ermana Ugona Societatis Iesu kapłana są opisane i przetłumaczone na cześć Bogu i Naświętszej Matce Jego* (Devotional sigh of the soul longing for God, intended for three wakes of men: for those converting to God, those enlightened by God, and those united with God, wherein the engravings of Herman Hugo's collection have been annotated and translated in honor of God and his most holy Mother). It draws the reader's attention to several elements: the title and author of the original, and the fact that he was a Jesuit; the change in the titles of the individual books and the resulting difference in the volume's concept; as well as the fact that the adaptation was not based on Hugo's elegies but the engravings featured in the original publication. It is worth mentioning that the manuscript copy left blank spaces

---

97   Manuscript kept at the Diocesan Library in Sandomierz, call no. A-99.

for the pasting of copperplate engravings, which were ultimately not included in the codex.

The essential part of the collection consists of the three books announced in its title, each of which contains fifteen poetic subscriptions. In this redaction, they are preceded by two rhymed works referred to as "figures": *Figura 1. abo Obraz początkowy od autora za tytuł tych trzech ksiąg położony* (Figure 1 or initial image, inserted by the author on the title of these three books), which is a subscription to the frontispiece known from the *Pia desideria* first edition, and *Figura 2. abo Obraz wtóry przed zaczęciem tych ksiąg położony* (Figure 2 or second image, inserted before the beginning of these books), which is a subscription to the initial engraving of the collection, originally marked as copperplate engraving zero.

The title of the original redaction was topped by a version of the well-known Jesuit motto: "Ad maiorem Dei gloriam et Beatissimae Virginis Mariae honorem" (To the greater glory of God, and to the honor of the Most Blessed Virgin Mary), while the second redaction was intended to add glory to the addressee to whom it was dedicated, that is, the widow Katarzyna Zasławska-Ostrogska (1634–94). It differs from the earlier version in being accompanied by a panegyric dedication and a four-line dedication to the Sobieski coat of arms, as well as by the omission of two texts, the one dedicated to the frontispiece and the one devoted to the engraving in the introductory emblem. The latter modification may have been prompted by technical considerations: only these two pieces were written in the Polish alexandrine (seven and six syllables), while the others were written in the hendecasyllable (five and six syllables). The decisive factor may also have been the fact that Mieleszko did not have these two engravings at his disposal and hence omitted the adjoining poems in the copy presented to the princess. For although the known copy of the second redaction[98] does not leave any space for the copperplate engravings, they may have been included in the clean copy gifted to the princess. This is suggested by the preface to the adaptation, in which the Jesuit poet recommends that his subscriptions be continuously confronted with the engravings, as well as the references to emblematic images found in his poetic texts.

In the second redaction, the title of the collection was modified to *Nabożne westchnienia, Duszy poczynającej, postępującej i doskonałej służące, od Hermana Hugona Societatis Iesu łacińskim wierszem, obrazami i naukami z doktorów ś[więtych] zebranemi wyrażone, a potym od jednego tegoż zakonu kapłana, na same obrazy i podpisy ich z Pisma Świętego wyjęte wzgląd mającego, wierszem*

---

98   Manuscript kept at the Library of the Russian Academy of Sciences in St. Petersburg, call no. O No 217.

polskim opisane roku Pańskiego 1657 (Devotional sighs, intended for the beginner, the proficient, and perfect Soul, by the Jesuit Herman Hugo expressed
in Latin verse, images, and teachings collected from the writings of the holy
doctors, and later by a certain priest of the same order, incorporating exclu-
sive engravings and their inscriptions as taken from the scriptures, drafted in
Polish verse in the year of our Lord 1657). Unlike the heading of the earlier
redaction, the second version stated that in the original book the emblems
were a four-component structure, consisting of verses, engravings, elegies, and
excerpts from the works of the doctors of the church, while Mieleszko's adaptation focused not only on the engravings but also on the biblical inscriptions
that underpinned them.

Both redactions were accompanied by a "Przedmowa do łaskawego
Czytelnika" (Preface to the gracious reader), in which Mieleszko expounded
on the concept of the three-book division used in the original. However, he
failed to mention Hugo's proposed affective adaptation of the three stages of
spiritual development, which he replaced with the classification into beginner,
proficient, and perfect in the service of God, popularized by Jesuit literature:

> Gracious reader, when inspecting the actions of people in the service of
> God, the spiritual fathers commonly divide them into three categories.
> Those who, attracted by the heavenly light, forsake the world's vanities
> and repent of their own volition for their past sins, in the world or in the
> order, are dubbed novices. Conversely, those who have already repaid the
> debt of their sins through penance and various ascetic practices and now
> exercise themselves in various virtues, are termed the proficient. Finally,
> those who are already well trained in the Christian virtues, especially in
> the queen of all virtues, the Divine Love, and whose only desire is to be
> dissolved from the flesh and immersed in God, so that they may eternally
> and without interruption partake of him, those, I say, are known as the
> perfect ones.[99]

In line with this explanation, Mieleszko expanded the title of his adaptation
and changed the original wording of the headings of each book to descriptive formulas of the following ilk: "Nabożnych westchnienia księga pierwsza,
ludziom pokutującym i do Boga nawracającym się abo, jako ojcowie duchowni
mówią, poczynającym służąca" (The first book of *Devotional Sighs* intended
for penitents and converts to God, or, as spiritual fathers call them, beginners).
Instead of affections, highlighted in Hugo's version, the confessor of Princess

---

99   Quotations from *Nabożne westchnienia* after Mieleszko, *Emblematy*.

Radziwiłł opted for the terminology used by the "spiritual fathers" and popularized by guidebooks on meditation, well known to his native audiences. For example, the six-volume opus by the Spanish Jesuit Luis de la Puente (1554–1624), *Meditationes de praecipuis fidei nostrae mysteriis* (Meditations on the fundamental mysteries of our faith), which was translated in 1621 for the Benedictine nuns of the Chełmno reform at the newly founded convent in Jarosław by their confessor, Jan Węgrzynkowic (d.1634), was based on a dual division of spiritual development into the beginners (*novissimi*), the proficient (*proficientes*), and the perfect (*perfecti*), on the one hand, and the corresponding stages of purification (*via purgativa*), enlightenment (*via illuminativa*), and union (*via unitiva*), on the other.[100] The same dual diagram as a synopsis for a collection of meditations, *Droga doskonałości chrześcijańskiej na trzy części rozłożona* (The way to christian perfection, divided into three parts), was used by Drużbicki, Mieleszko's novice-master in Kraków.[101] Princess Katarzyna's confessor brought the first of these divisions to the fore. Such a clear departure from the affective titles of Hugo's books represented a significant change and the first step toward a stronger subordination of Mieleszko's adaptation to argumentation that appeals to the intellect, so essential to the practice of spiritual exercises. Other solutions in his adaptation likewise veered in this direction.

In presenting the composition of Hugo's emblems—which spelled out the religious matter of the collection through quotations from exegetical writings, elegies, and engravings—Mieleszko focused on the latter most, considering them the most attractive medium of the original print. He invoked the authority of Horace, while the passage about how it is easier to understand by looking than by listening (*De arte poetica* I, vv. 180–81) may have been drawn from Otto van Veen's introduction to the collection of *Emblemata Horatiana* (Horatian emblems), where it was quoted for the very same reason.[102] The nature of Mieleszko's adaptation is determined by him giving primacy to the visual medium. In the preface, Mieleszko stated that since someone else had already undertaken the translation of Hugo's elegies, therefore—unwilling to get in the other's way—he chose to limit himself to a poetic elaboration of the inscriptions and engravings. Whether this explanation was true is difficult to determine (the translation referred to by Mieleszko is not known today).

---

100   Luis de la Puente, *Rozmyślania o tajemnicach wiary naszej*, trans. Jan Węgrzynkowic (Jarosław: Jan Szeliga, 1621), 1:fol. 1ʳ.

101   Kasper Drużbicki, *Droga doskonałości chrześcijańskiej na trzy części rozłożona* (Kalisz: Kolegium Jezuickie, 1665), fols. a4ᵛ–b1ᵛ.

102   Otto van Veen, *Lectori seu spectatori*, in van Veen, *Q. Horati Flacci emblemata* (Antwerp: Hieronymus Verdussen, 1607), 6.

Considering the parts of the introduction favoring the engravings over the other components of the *Pia desideria* emblems, the possibility cannot be excluded that mentioning the projected translation was merely Mieleszko's excuse, since he was not so much interested in translating the Latin elegies as in using the inscriptions and engravings for meditative purposes.

The text of each Polish emblem consists of three elements: a single-sentence presentation of the engraving, the author's translation of the verse constituting the inscription, and a poetic subscription of between fourteen and twenty-eight lines. The presence of the first of these elements in both redactions proves that Mieleszko correctly assumed that most copies of his work would be devoid of engravings. The latter redaction of the collection differs from the earlier one not only in its literary framework (a different wording of the title, an added dedication and poem on the Sobieski coat of arms, two omitted introductory poems) but also in the somewhat different development of the poetic subscriptions. Compared to the original edition, the poet condensed the descriptions of the engravings, where he limited any volubility, while expanding their length when it served to illuminate spiritual explications. He also occasionally exchanged neutral wording for expressions of greater affective power, as for example in the couplet concerning the loss of time: "Wnet stanie w myśli, jak wielem strawiła / Czasu, kiedym się marnością bawiła" (I shall instantly think of the time I have wasted on vanities), which he replaced with a vision of horror at the thought of the final judgment (I, 13, vv. 13–18): "Stanie mi wnetże na myśli sąd srogi, / Stanie czas marnie utracony drogi, / Którym na świeckich marnościach trawiła, / A na zbawienie najmniej nie robiła. / Pocznie mi serce od żalu się krajać, / Pocznę mdleć, pocznę jak wosk w ogniu tajać" (I shall instantly think of the dreadful judgment and the precious time I have wasted on secular vanities instead of tending to my salvation. My heart shall be bursting with grief, I shall falter, I shall melt like wax in the fire).

The sparse rewording introduced by Mieleszko to the latter redaction of his collection clearly improved its artistic quality.

3.2.3 Zbigniew Morsztyn's Adaptation

Although Princess Katarzyna made no efforts to publish the emblem books dedicated to her by Mieleszko, his writings must have appealed to her, so much so that when the opportunity arose a dozen years later, she commissioned a similar series from one of the most outstanding poets of the Polish baroque, Zbigniew Morsztyn.[103] Morsztyn's published pieces were limited to a total of

---

103   For biographical data concerning Zbigniew Morsztyn, see Janusz Pelc, *Zbigniew Morsztyn: Arianin i poeta* (Wrocław: Zakład Narodowy im. Ossolińskich, 1966).

three minor works and one funerary collection; however, his lyrical output, which was circulated in the form of handwritten copies, was extensive. The unique character of the author's work was determined, on the one hand, by his experience as a soldier and, on the other, by his activity as a member of the Minor Reformed Church of Poland (Polish Brethren or Arians). The former translated into the explicitness of wartime lyricism, the latter into the deep spirituality of his religious works.

Morsztyn came from a noble family of Arians with a seat in Podgórze. As a young man, he affiliated himself with the Lithuanian court of the Radziwiłł family, in whose service he remained for the rest of his life. In 1653, he took part in an expedition against an uprising of the Zaporizhian Cossacks, which was when his earliest datable poems were written. A year later, he fought against Russian forces in the Battle of Shepeleviche (present-day Belarus), where his unit was routed, many of his comrades falling in combat. Morsztyn lamented their loss in an extensive series of epitaphs. In 1657, during the Polish–Swedish war, he was taken prisoner in Swedish-occupied Kraków, another fact he commemorated in his poetry.

In 1658, the Sejm passed a law ordering the Polish Brethren to convert or leave the territory of the Polish–Lithuanian state under penalty of death. In the wake of the newly adopted law, Morsztyn emigrated to the Duchy of Prussia. Here, in the leased estate of Rudówka (present-day Stara Rudówka), he established an Arian congregation that became a thriving center of religious and social life for the exiles.

When, after Bogusław Radziwiłł's (1620–69) death, his then two-year-old daughter, Princess Ludwika Karolina (1667–95), became heiress to his fortune, Michał Kazimierz Radziwiłł was named one of Ludwika's legal guardians, while Morsztyn was appointed one of the administrators overseeing the orphan's latifundia. These events took place in the early 1670s, and as a result of the new client relations thus forged, Michał Kazimierz's wife was now in a position to commission a new collection of emblems. Morsztyn reported the commission in an annotation preceding the work, noting that the poems for the engravings and inscriptions of the collection by a certain Capuchin friar were written at the behest of the princess. The commission specified the nature of the undertaking: the emblems were to be original compositions inspired by the engravings and their biblical inscriptions. By revealing the nature of the order, Morsztyn no longer had to account for his choice of adaptation strategy, which was something that Mieleszko still felt obliged to do.

Morsztyn's annotation reveals that the author of the collection that served as a basis for the adaptation was a Capuchin friar. The book in question was titled *Les emblemes d'amour divin et humain ensemble: Expliquez par des vers françois par un pere capucin* (Emblems of the divine and human love together:

explained in a French verse by a Capuchin father).[104] It was likely written by Ludovicus van Leuven, born Philippe de Vilers (d.1661), son of a professor of medicine at the University of Leuven, who joined the Order of Capuchin Friars Minor in 1622.[105]

Comprising 118 engravings, the first edition of the collection was published in 1631 in the Paris printing house of Jean Messager (c.1572–1649). Morsztyn used the second edition, expanded with an additional engraving (it corresponds to emblem 5 in the Polish version), printed after Pierre Mariette I (d.1657) took over as the owner of the printing house in 1637. The differences between the reprint and the first edition are not limited to the addition of a single emblem. In the *editio princeps*, each engraving bore a French title and a poetic subscription of three quatrains by the Capuchin author. The re-issue omitted these elements, focusing only on the copies of copperplate engravings, and it is therefore limited to those textual segments that were integral to the engravings, that is, the Latin inscriptions and short subscriptions in the form of French couplets.

Of the 119 engravings from the original edition, Morsztyn furnished 113 with poetic elaborations (as a matter of fact, the total number of poems amounts to 114, as one of the engravings has two variations in Morsztyn's cycle), and their order is different from that known from the Capuchin's print. Thus, it is possible that the French collection came into the poet's hands in the form of loose sheets. This would explain both the lack of development of some of the engravings in the adaptation (a loose card is easier to misplace) and the disruption of the original layout of the collection.[106]

Although the princess commissioned Morsztyn to adapt a different volume than the one she had received from Mieleszko, his work nevertheless had much in common with *Pia desideria*. The volume edited by the Capuchin author was a compilation of emblematic engravings from several collections. Quite a few engravings therein were borrowed from such bestsellers as *Amoris Divini emblemata* (1615) by Otto van Veen or *Amoris Divini et humani antipathia sive effectus varii* (Aversion between God's and human love, or various implications; 1629), while individual images were taken from the volumes *Typus mundi, in quo eius calamitates et pericula nec non divini, humanique amoris anthipatia emblematice proponuntur* (An image of the world in which its misfortunes and dangers, and indeed aversion between divine and human love,

---

104 Mary Wanda Stephen, "Do biografii i twórczości Zbigniewa Morsztyna," *Pamiętnik literacki* 54, no. 4 (1963): 415–42, here 429–34, 442; Pelc, *Zbigniew Morsztyn*, 252–56, 395–400.

105 Karel Porteman, "Nieuwe gegevens over de drukgeschiedenis, de bronnen en de auteur van de embleembundel *Amoris divini et humani antipathia*," *Ons geestelijk erf* 49 (1975): 193–213, here 201–2.

106 Stephen, "Do biografii," 434–35.

are emblematically represented; 1627) and *Passio Domini nostri Jesu Christi*
(Passion of our Lord Jesus Christ; n.d.); the second edition also includes an
engraving from Hoyer's print *Flammulae amoris s[ancti] p[atris] Augustini*
(Little flames of love by the holy father Augustine; 1629). The Capuchin author
also appended the volume with engravings modeled on the forty-six copperplates by Bolswert, commissioned for *Pia desideria*, although he slightly
changed the original order in which they had been arranged.[107]

Morsztyn's adaptation accounts for most of the engravings from the
Capuchin's volume, but not all of them. Among those omitted are four engravings originally included in *Pia desideria* (I, 9, II, 8, 9, III, 11). This means that
he elaborated as many as forty-two of the original forty-six images poetically.
In the Polish collection, they were shuffled with others, thus forming a newly
composed entity; however, they nevertheless give an idea of how Morsztyn
interpreted the biblically determined engravings from Hugo's volume.

TABLE 1   Breakdown of engravings from Herman Hugo's *Pia desideria*, as included in
             Zbigniew Morsztyn's collection

Hugo	Morsztyn	Hugo	Morsztyn	Hugo	Morsztyn
0	101	II, 1	26	III, 1	111
I, 1	57	II, 2	24	III, 2	23
I, 2	106	II, 3	27	III, 3	18
I, 3	107	II, 4	25	III, 4	53
I, 4	81	II, 5	75	III, 5	52
I, 5	113	II, 6	78	III, 6	89
I, 6	84	II, 7	108	III, 7	3
I, 7	110	II, 8	–	III, 8	88
I, 8	21	II, 9	–	III, 9	2
I, 9	–	II, 10	39	III, 10	85
I, 10	20	II, 11	34	III, 11	–
I, 11	49	II, 12	40	III, 12	46
I, 12	32	II, 13	64	III, 13	80
I, 13	47	II, 14	112	III, 14	94
I, 14	96	II, 15	100	III, 15	65
I, 15	29				

---

107   Stephen, "Do biografii," 429–34, 442; Pelc, *Zbigniew Morsztyn*, 395–400.

Was the poet aware that some of the copperplates of the Capuchin's compilation collection were copies of engravings from *Pia desideria*? The question has been posed several times, invariably without eliciting an answer.[108] In fact, such an answer can be provided: there is no doubt that Morsztyn was familiar with the book by the Dutch Jesuit and studied it carefully. It is evident from those paragraphs of his subscriptions that, although not motivated by either engravings or biblical inscriptions, do have their counterparts in Hugo's elegies. For example, in poem 75, written to accompany the equivalent of the engraving of emblem II, 5, the Polish poet enumerated three Old Testament exempla proving that eyesight can be a source of grave sin (e.g., the old men peeping at Susanna [Dan. 13], or that of David peeping at Bathsheba [2 Sm. 11:2–12:25], as well as the young Dinah admiring finely dressed women [Gen. 34]). All three examples echoed Hugo's elegy (vv. 25–32), which in turn drew inspiration from a passage from Pseudo-Bernard's *Liber de modo bene vivendi ad sororem* (The book on how to live a good life, for the sister; 23,69), included in Hugo's commentary to this emblem.

Morsztyn's familiarity with *Pia desideria* is also indicated in the presentations of the engravings, annotated subsequently. For example, emblem 113 was captioned with a description: "The potter's wheel bears an incipient vessel, with various other vessels standing on the sides."[109] In the Capuchin's collection, the copies of the engravings were stripped of their backgrounds, and so, in this case, they do not depict any vessels other than the one formed on the potter's wheel. Conversely, Bolswert's copperplate engraving for emblem I, 5 in *Pia desideria* features more than a dozen clay human silhouettes standing on two shelves, and it is the reminiscence of that very engraving that was included in Morsztyn's description (fig. 3). It is worth noting that the Polish poet had the original engraving in mind, and not its equivalent, which was introduced into polygraphic circulation by van Haestens in the 1628 edition, where the scene was set out in the open, and thus it, too, missed the shelves filled with finished dishes. These examples prove that Morsztyn was not only aware of the syncretic nature of the collection he was commissioned to elaborate but was also intimately familiar with the *Pia desideria* volume, both with respect to Hugo's elegies and Bolswert's suggestive copperplates.

Morsztyn's collection of emblems has survived in three handwritten copies. Two of them—a copy of the poet's oeuvre compiled in 1680–81, titled *Muza*

---

108   Stephen, "Do biografii," 435; Pelc, *Zbigniew Morsztyn*, 260; Pfeiffer, "*Pobożne pragnienia*," 16.
109   Quotations from Morsztyn's emblems after Zbigniew Morsztyn, *Emblemata*, ed. Janusz and Paulina Pelc (Warsaw: Neriton, 2001).

Memento, quæso, quod sicut lutum feceris me,
et in puluerem reduces me! Job. 10.
                                                                    5.

FIGURE 3   Boëtius à Bolswert, engraving no. 5 (I, 5) in: Herman Hugo, *Pia desideria*
            (Antwerp: Hendrik Aertssens, 1624). Amsterdam, Rijksmuseum

domowa (Domestic muse),[110] and the so-called Radziwiłłs manuscript[111]—include all poems from the collection, along with the author's dedication. The third codex, a handwritten poetic collection from the last quarter of the seventeenth century, contains an early redaction of the first two emblems, in addition to six other poems written by Morsztyn between 1674 and 1678.[112] The version recorded here differs from the final version by a number of stylistic variations in the text, as well as a distich that was elided from the first emblem after the poet chose to use it as part of the dedication to Princess Radziwiłł in the final redaction of the volume (vv. 19–20).

What is more interesting are the differences documenting the change in Morsztyn's adaptive strategy. In the final version of the cycle, the Latin inscriptions from the original (usually in the form of verses from the Vulgate) are translated into Polish; it also omits the subscription couplets in French by the Capuchin friar. In contrast, an early redaction of the first two emblems includes two types of text copied from the engravings of *Les emblemes d'Amour Divin et humain ensemble* (i.e., Latin verses and French couplets). In both cases, the couplets have their counterparts in Morsztyn's poetic arrangement. The content of the latter was paraphrased by the poet at the beginning of the emblematic subscription (2, vv. 1–2), while the content of the former was amplified to eight verses (1, vv. 3–6, 13–16). This is worth emphasizing, since the subsequent works of Morsztyn's collection usually lack equally explicit references to the French couplets.

The change in Morsztyn's adaptation strategy must have come under the influence of his principal, who had no command of either Latin or French. It was probably for this reason that the princess gave the order, as reported by Morsztyn, to arrange Polish poems inspired solely by biblical inscriptions and their pictorial representations, disregarding the French couplets. Katarzyna Radziwiłł wished for the new collection to be compiled in the same way as Mieleszko's adaptations that she had enjoyed so much.

The commission was executed as such. Ultimately, Morsztyn's emblems consist of the same elements we know from Mieleszko's adaptation: a single-sentence description of the engraving, the author's translation of a Vulgate verse, and a poetic subscription containing between fourteen and twenty-six lines (two subscriptions are longer, standing at forty and forty-six lines, respectively; however, given the short meter in the copies, two verses were transcribed in a single line, and hence the length of these two subscriptions is comparable to

---

110   The manuscript kept at the Library of the Ossoliński National Institute in Wrocław, call no. 5547/II, 91–191 (P.609).
111   Manuscript kept at the National Library in Warsaw, call no. II 6803, fols. 1ʳ–58ᵛ (P.609).
112   Manuscript kept at the National Library in Warsaw, call no. Akc. 13102, fol. 8ʳ–8ᵛ.

the others). Such an arrangement strictly corresponds to the preceding collection by Mieleszko, even if it was apparently not obvious to Morsztyn.

In addition to translating the Latin verses into Polish and omitting the French subscriptions, Morsztyn had to supplement the emblems with a description of the engravings. He did this upon completion of his work, when he no longer had access to the Capuchin's print, and as such his presentations oftentimes miss the mark. For example, Morsztyn's emblem 64 was composed for an engraving modeled on the *Pia desideria* copperplate (II, 13), showing a boy (personification of the Holy Love) carrying a girl (personification of the Soul) on his back, the latter holding an anchor. Morsztyn described the engraving as follows: "A man tramples on crowns and other splendid objects and riches, his eyes turning to heaven." Descriptions that are either completely inconsistent with the engravings—as is the case with this one—or deviate from them in terms of details, are numerous in Morsztyn's collection. The poet drew them up, relying not so much on his memory as on the descriptive passages of his own subscriptions (in this case, he used vv. 1–8 of the emblem, cautioning the reader against trusting the hypocritical world and its charms). And since he remembered engravings from various emblematic collections, matching the right one to each poetic description often proved impossible. Thus, it is evident that aligning the various emblematic elements to the template of Mieleszko's cycle came at a price.

The timeline of Morsztyn's work on the collection has so far been determined with little precision—"completed in 1675–1680 or 1676–1680, possibly starting in the 1660s, likely also revised after 1680."[113] In fact, the timeline can be narrowed down to a great extent. The dedication preceding the collection refers to the election of Jan III Sobieski as king of Poland on May 21, 1674, as a recent event. The dedication must have been written after the princess's brother was elected ruler and before his coronation of February 2, 1676, which Morsztyn fails to mention. This time frame can be narrowed down further.

In late June/early July 1675, with his eyes set on publication, the poet sent the finished text of the collection to his friend Kazimierz Krzysztof Kłokocki (c.1625–85), who managed the Radziwiłł printing house in Slutsk. It is only Kłokocki's letters that have survived to document the exchange of correspondence on the matter. On July 15, Kłokocki confirmed the receipt of the manuscript, reporting that he had not yet reviewed it for lack of time, although the very person to whom the collection was dedicated made it print-worthy. He also stressed that he would like the book to be published with engravings. In another letter, Kłokocki stated that he had familiarized himself with the collection and concluded that it was definitely worth publishing. He also reminded Morsztyn that the engravings would increase the value of the publication.

---

113   Pelc, *Zbigniew Morsztyn*, 361.

Morsztyn was to notify the printer promptly if he was interested in including them in the volume; otherwise, the typesetting process would commence immediately.[114]

The collection of emblems was thus completed before July 1675, and it was only Kłokocki's efforts to procure the engravings that may have prolonged the book's publication. Starting in 1674, Kłokocki endeavored to acquire a Polish translation of Paul Rycaut's (1629–1700) *Histoire de l'état présent de l'empire Ottoman* (The history of the present state of the Ottoman empire), and it was likely as early as then that he sought to collaborate with the talented copperplate engraver Maxim Vashchenko (d.1708) of Mogilev, who, based on the French edition of Rycaut's collection, made copies of nineteen engravings for its Polish translation, published in Slutsk.[115] Said engraver could be also entrusted with the preparation of the copperplate copies of engravings intended for Morsztyn's book.

For reasons unknown, the collection was not printed. This is a great pity, because, from the artistic standpoint, had Kłokocki indeed procured the engravings, the publication would have made for the most interesting Polish emblem book of the seventeenth century.

3.2.4 The Meditative Nature and Poetic Elaboration of Mieleszko's and Morsztyn's Adaptations

The poetic adaptations by the Jesuit Mieleszko and the Arian Morsztyn were subordinated to the rigor of methodical meditation, which, although promoted mainly by members of the Society of Jesus, was also popular among Evangelicals and the Polish Brethren. In the texts that serve as the literary brace of the collection, this aspect was not highlighted. Mieleszko brushed it off with silence, while Morsztyn's rhymed dedication designated his emblems as meditations on the Divine Love (v. 15), without delving deeper into this thread. The lack of explicit introductory statements about the meditative nature of the adaptation can be taken as evidence of the universal appeal of this type of text.

The Ignatian way of meditating involved three mental faculties: memory, intellect, and will. Memory helped visualize the scene constituting the subject of meditation. The intellect contemplated the significance of the scene and used it to extract the relevant moral teachings. The process was crowned by acts of will, taking the form of thanksgiving, petition, worship, or entrusting oneself to God. In the spiritual exercises designed according to the above formula, a key role was played by *compositio loci*, a suggestive visualization that disciplined the mind, facilitated concentration, and served as the subject of

---

114   Pelc, *Zbigniew Morsztyn*, 227–28.
115   Jolanta Talbierska, *Grafika XVII wieku w Polsce: Funkcje, ośrodki, artyści, dzieła* (Warsaw: Neriton, 2011), 101–2.

meditation. The Jesuits soon discovered that engravings were an excellent aid in imagining the scene that was the subject of a spiritual exercise. Thus, illustrated collections of religiously themed emblems proved to be an ideal tool for fostering meditative practices.[116]

The aforementioned layout of the spiritual exercise is discernible in the subscriptions of both Mieleszko[117] and Morsztyn.[118] The meditation promoted by Loyola distinguished between four main stages: preparation, imagination or visualization, consideration, and prayer. Preparation (*praeparatio*) involved focusing one's mind and tuning it toward a conversation with God. Morsztyn alludes to this stage in the dedication of his collection, where he writes about abandoning secular thoughts and affairs that preoccupy mind, since his works were to be the subject of meditative reading (vv. 21–26).

The second stage (*repraesentatio*) involved visualizing the relevant scene. In religious emblematic collections of a meditative nature, assistance in this respect was provided by an engraving, with the poetic subscriptions written for Princess Radziwiłł serving as its lyrical description, sometimes complemented by a hint pointing to the graphic character of the visualized scene, both in Mieleszko's text, "Nigdym w tak ciężkim nie postała razie, / **Jaki w tym widzisz nieszczęsnym obrazie**" (Never have I found myself in as dire a predicament **as the one you see depicted in this terrible engraving**; I, 9, vv. 1–2), and in that by Morsztyn: "Gdzieżem i w jakim **widzę się** więzieniu? / Żyję czym w śmierci położony cieniu?" (Where am I and what prison **do I see myself** in? Am I alive, or have I been laid in mortal darkness?; 85 [= *Pia desideria* III, 10], vv. 1–2).

Another stage of meditation was the consideration of the meanings behind the visualized scene, subordinated to the reader's intellect (*consideratio*). This phase could be accompanied by strong emotions, either positive or negative, depending on the subject of the spiritual exercise. Said emotions facilitated greater involvement in intellectual analysis. At the level of the poetic subscriptions, this part corresponds to the exegesis of the scene depicted in the engraving. By way of example, it is worth citing the subscriptions accompanying emblem I, 2, whose inscription is the verse, "O God, thou knowest my foolishness and my

---

116 See, e.g., Ralph Dekoninck, Ad Imaginem: *Statuts, fonctions et usages de l'image dans la littérature spirituelle jésuite du XVIIᵉ siècle* (Geneva: Droz, 2005).

117 Joanna Hałoń, "Wobec obrazu," *Zeszyty naukowe Katolickiego Uniwersytetu Lubelskiego* 46, nos. 1/2 (2003): 33–61, here 50–56; Grześkowiak and Niedźwiedź, *Wstęp*, 64–69.

118 David J. Welsh, "Zbigniew Morsztyn's Poetry of Meditation," *Slavic and East European Journal* 9, no. 1 (1965): 56–61; Krzysztof Mrowcewicz, "'O miłości Bożej rozmyślanie': O *Emblematach* Zbigniewa Morsztyna," in *Literatura i kultura polska po "potopie"*, ed. Barbara Otwinowska, Janusz Pelc, and Barbara Falęcka (Wrocław: Zakład Narodowy im. Ossolińskich, 1992), 153–64.

Deus tu scis insipientiam meam, et delicta mea à te non sunt abscondita. Psal. 68.

FIGURE 4   Boëtius à Bolswert, engraving no. 2 (1, 2) in: Herman Hugo, *Pia desideria* (Antwerp: Hendrik Aertssens, 1624). Amsterdam, Rijksmuseum

offences are not hidden from thee" (Ps. 68:5; fig. 4). In the quotations, I indicate the passages in the engraving's description (in bold) and its explication (italics). The opening of Mieleszko's subscription (1, 2, vv. 1–10) reads as follows:

> Dobrze **zasłania oczy na twe sprawy**
> **Bóg, widząc w tobie dziecinne zabawy.**
> *Dzieciom igrzyska służą takie małym,*
> *Którzy są w wieku jeszcze niedojźrałym:*
> **Wiatraczki nosić, na koniczki wsiadać,**
> **Czaczkami głowę i ręce okładać.**
> *Już takich igrzysk zapominać mają*
> *Ci, co na służbę Boską się udają;*
> *Już im statecznych trzeba obyczajów,*
> *Nie płochych jakich dziecinnych zwyczajów.*

> Rightly **does God cover his eyes at the sight of your childish games.** *Such plays only befit young children, who are still immature*: **to carry pinwheels, to ride a rocking horse, to adorn one's head and hands with toys.** *Such plays are to be forgotten by those who choose to serve God, for what they need is maturity, not reckless childlike behavior.*

In turn, Mieleszko's subscription opens with the following words (106, vv. 1–12):

> Gdyby śmiertelnym mogła być widziana
> Dusza ma okiem, jako jest ubrana,
> **Jakie pstrociny, jakie śmieszne kroje,**
> **Jakie dziecinne i błazeńskie stroje,**
> *W które ją grzechy nieszczęsne ubrały*
> *I na szyderstwo szczyre ją podały,*
> Pewnie by od tak brzydkiego widziadła
> Zgorzała z wstydu i w ziemię przepadła.
> Ale to gorsza, że *te takie fraszki*
> *Wiecznej ją Twojej pozbawiają łaski,*
> *Że się jej wstydzisz* i że słusznie **dłonią**
> **Twą świętą oczy Twoje się zasłonią.**

> If the carnal eye could see how my Soul is clad, **in what garish motley, in what ludicrous attire, in what childish and jester-like garments** *it is dressed by the damned sins, exposing itself to mockery*, she would likely burn

with shame and sink beneath the ground at so unpleasant a sight. Worse still, however, *such playthings strip her of your eternal favor and cause you to be ashamed of her* and rightly **veil your eyes with your holy hand**.

In both cases, the description of the scene shown in the engraving was seamlessly combined with its interpretation. Mieleszko sometimes separates the descriptive and analytical parts, while Morsztyn prefers to fuse them together; however, in general, the synthesis of these two measures is shared by both poets.

The Jesuit model of meditation distinguished one more element, that is, prayer (*oratio*), during which the orans, ignited by their inner fervor, talks to God or Christ, as if he were present before them. The final element of the spiritual exercise is an act of will, whose counterpart in the poetic subscriptions was the final appeal addressed to God, his Son, the Divine Love, or the Soul. In the subscription to emblem I, 2, Mieleszko formulated such an appeal using the following wording (I, 2, vv. 15–18): "Statek rad w Duszy i przystojność widzi / Bóg, a takowych igrzysk nienawidzi, / Przetoż Mu z lepszym stawiaj się widokiem, / A wnet wesołym pojźry na cię okiem" (God looks favorably on the stateliness and decency of the Soul, and he hates this game, therefore let him see your better side, and he will instantly see you in a more favorable way). In turn, Morsztyn put it as follows (106, vv. 13–18): "Zbawicielu mój, niechże przez Twe święte / Ręce będą z niej te ubiory zdjęte, / A w bisior oblecz ją sprawiedliwości / I niezmazanej biały len czystości, / Perły cnót świętych, skruchy zausznice / Niech stroje Twojej będą służebnice" (My Savior, may your holy hands strip her [my Soul] of these garments, and dress it with the fabric of righteousness and a linen robe of unblemished whiteness; may your servant be adorned with the pearls of holy virtues and the earrings of repentance).

The difference in the content and address of the appeals—Mieleszko's plea was addressed to the Soul, whom it implored to settle down and thereby appease God's wrath, while Morsztyn's was directed to Christ, whom he urged to restrain the unruly Soul and clothe it in a way that would please him—resulted from different interpretations of the same scene, already evident in the descriptions of the images written by the two poets. Each emphasized a different aspect: according to Mieleszko, God rebukes the Soul's frivolous habits, urging it toward constancy, while Morsztyn only mentioned the Soul's clownish attire, omitting the reaction of the personified Divine Love.

Both artists tended to fill the common framework of the meditative segments with different poetic matter. Mieleszko focused on the accurate description and analysis of the engravings, while Morsztyn was more eager to showcase his erudition (primarily biblical, but also with respect to the ancient classics).

Mieleszko's meticulous inspection of graphic details and his brilliant ability to interpret the perceived nuances is commendable. One notable example is his interpretation of the meaning of the telescope through which the Soul gazes at the ultimate things in the image of emblem I, 14. According to Morsztyn, the engraving depicts an encouragement for the distracted Soul to see things on the horizon that she does not care to consider on a daily basis (emblem 96). What Mieleszko noticed, however, is that the Soul holds the telescope in reverse, so that instead of magnifying the ultimate matters, it creates the illusion of their remoteness (I, 14, vv. 6–12). For Morsztyn, the image presented the scene as it should have been (wise is the Soul that discerns what lies afar), while Mieleszko saw it as a portrayal of the heroine's thoughtlessness (imprudent is the Soul that deceives itself). It should be noted that the reversal of the telescope was not mentioned by Hugo in the elegy, let alone by the authors of the exegetical excerpts he collected. Mieleszko spotted more such significant details in his subscriptions to Bolswert's miniature engravings.

Mieleszko occasionally made the biblical inscriptions of the emblems his literary matter and opened his poem with their paraphrases. An accumulation of such cases can be found in the last book of his collection.

In the preface, Mieleszko stated that he did not intend to translate the Latin elegies but would confine himself to a lyrical analysis of Bolswert's illustrations. This is not to say, however, that he did not read Hugo's poems. He used them readily, as long as they helped him interpret the details he noticed in the engravings. In his adaptation, he often drew attention to the background details of the image, which he used as an element of comparison. In the engraving of emblem I, 9, the personifications of sins drive the Soul into a net, which is tightened by Death hidden in the shadow of a tree. Since the tree branches are overhung with a spider's web, Mieleszko concluded that the devil attacks the Soul like a spider attacks a fly when it falls into its web (vv. 11–14). In an analogous fashion (i.e., for comparative purposes), Mieleszko used the bucking horse and resting ox shown in the background of image II, 1 (vv. 13–16), the shoot entwined around the trunk in the foreground of engraving II, 12 (vv. 13–16), or the boy with a tethered bird in the backdrop of engraving III, 9 (vv. 13–16). None of these comparisons were of his own invention; each time he adopted them from Hugo's elegies (I, 9, vv. 45–46; II, 1, vv. 17–24; II, 12, vv. 75–78; III, 9, vv. 67–74). Mieleszko used the rhymed verses of the original merely as clues for the interpretation of the engravings. He was otherwise unconcerned with Hugo's elaborate elegies.

Morsztyn, too, was fond of opening his subscriptions with the biblical inscription. In his case, however, this was part of a broader strategy of tapping into the text of the scriptures as poetic matter. He wove the biblical verses so densely into his own subscriptions that some even resemble biblical centos. For example, the emblem corresponding to image I, 10 in *Pia desideria*, accompanied by the inscription, "Enter not into judgment with thy servant, for in thy sight no man living shall be justified" (Ps. 142:2), opens with a paraphrase of said biblical verse (vv. 1–2): "Nie wchodź, o Boże, Boże litościwy, / W sąd z winowajcą Twoim sprawiedliwy" (Merciful God, do not subject the guilty to your righteous judgment). This is immediately followed by several more verses from the scriptures (vv. 6–12): "Wiem, że na liczbie zostałem Ci więcéj / Winien talentów niż dziesięć tysięcy. / Dług to jest wielki, dług niewypłacony, / Godzienem tego, żebym był wrzucony / W wieczne więzienie i nie wyszedł z niego, / Aż do pieniążka oddam ostatniego" (I know that my debt exceeds ten thousand talents. It is a great debt, an unpayable debt, I deserve to be thrown into eternal prison and shall not come out thence, till I have paid the uttermost farthing).

The first two lines are an allusion to the opening of Jesus's parable of the unforgiving debtor: "And when he had begun to take the account, one was brought to him that owed him ten thousand talents" (Matt. 18:24). The next four allude to a thread from the Sermon on the Mount, concerning the reckoning of one's sins at the divine judgment: "Be at agreement with thy adversary betimes, whilst thou art in the way with him; lest perhaps the adversary deliver thee to the judge [...] and thou be cast into prison. Amen I say to thee: Thou shalt not go out from thence till thou repay the last farthing" (Matt. 5:25–26). Morsztyn evokes the biblical phrases so faithfully that one can clearly spot the lexical borrowings from the Polish translation of the Vulgate by the Jesuit Jakub Wujek (1541–97), the important Catholic translation of the scriptures (1599) that molded biblical Polish for the next three centuries.

The second way of using passages from the Bible was as a reservoir of instructive examples. In the subscriptions to engravings taken from *Pia desideria*, Morsztyn often showed off his non-obvious (i.e., not suggested by the inscription or engraving) biblical erudition. In the poem accompanying the engraving of emblem I, 13 (47, vv. 19–21), Morsztyn mentions the miraculous ten-degree retraction of the sundial shadow, a mark of King Hezekiah's healing (Isa. 38:7–8); in the subscription to emblem II, 14 (112, vv. 5–6), the poet evokes the plant whose shadow shielded the prophet Jonah (Jonah 4:6–7); in the verses to emblem III, 10 (85, vv. 8–12), Morsztyn refers to the imprisonment of young Joseph (Gen. 39:1–20) and King Manasseh (2 Chron. 33:11), in the latter case paraphrasing a verse of the apocryphal Prayer of Manasseh, included in Wujek's translation of the scriptures.

Commissioned by the Catholic princess Radziwiłł, Morsztyn's emblematic collection was a compilation of engravings designed by a Catholic friar, while his choice of biblical paraphrases was based on Wujek's Catholic translation into Polish. However, Mortsztyn's freedom in using excerpts from the Bible indicates his background as a Polish Brother with a profound knowledge of the scriptures.

Morsztyn's erudition was not limited to the Bible. He boldly tapped into secular subjects, too, as long as they were linked to the topic of his interest. In keeping with this principle, Morsztyn's subscription to the equivalent of emblem II, 13 includes the information about the days of the kingfisher (i.e., two windless weeks on the Sicilian Sea [64, vv. 21–22]), which he had read about in Pliny's (23–79 CE) *Natural History* (10,49,90); similarly, when composing a commentary on engraving III, 5, Morsztyn mentions a salamander that dwells in fire (52, vv. 11–14). In the same vein, the main source of the subscription to emblem III, 10 (80, vv. 3–4 and 9–14) was the characterization of the Iron Age borrowed from Ovid's *Metamorphoses* (I, vv. 129–31 and 144–50). One would search in vain for similar solutions in Mieleszko's collection.

The two authors commissioned to write emblems for Princess Radziwiłł had distinctly different poetic temperaments. Mieleszko was more disciplined and composed his subscriptions more consistently. Morsztyn, confident in his lyrical experience, was more willing to experiment with creative matter (for example, one of his subscriptions is a reworking of his earlier erotic poem). Also, the scale of emotions embedded in poetic subscriptions is more extensive in the adaptation by Morsztyn, who readily reached for exclamation points and dramatic rhetorical questions, an approximation to the solutions proposed by Hugo. Conversely, Mieleszko's works are more muted and economical in terms of his choice of poetic measures. His subscriptions focus primarily on a verbal reproduction of the engraving, one that would not miss any detail to provide the viewer with a reliable foundation for their meditative reflections.

3.3   Subscriptions in Engravings of Prints

The adaptations discussed in this and the following subsection amount to merely one minor subscription, and thus from the point of view of any quantitative research they are meaningless. But since in both cases they represent an important category of reception, they are worthy of some further attention.

One form of adapting Latin emblem books to the needs of domestic readers was through the addition of vernacular subscriptions. This practice was also known in the Polish–Lithuanian state. Only a handful of prints containing such emblem adaptations have survived: Georg Oemler's (1517–69) collection of vanitas emblems *Icones mortis* (Images of death) from 1547; Jacob Cats's erotic emblem book *Silenus Alcibiadis sive Proteus* (Silenus of Alcibiades, or Proteus) from around 1622; Georgette de Montenay's (1540–81) religious emblem collection *Emblematum christianorum centuria* (A century of Christian emblems) from 1584; and Luzvic's volume of emblems *Cor Deo devotum Iesu pacifici Salomonis thronus regius* from 1628.[119] In one of the religious emblem books centered on the topic of spousal mysticism that has survived until today, a seventeenth-century Polish author incorporated subscriptions of his own creation after each original sestina. Said book is a copy of *Amoris Divini et humani effectus varii, sacrae scripturae, sanctorumque p[atrum] sententiis ac Gallicis versibus illustrati* (Different effects of divine and human love, illustrated with passages from the holy scriptures and the holy fathers, as well as with French rhymes), published in 1626 and kept at the Library of the University of Uppsala.

The pages featuring engravings and a transcript of Polish subscriptions were rendered available to researchers by Paulina Buchwald-Pelcowa (1934–2021) and Janusz Pelc (1930–2005).[120] One shortcoming of this useful edition is the thesis advocated by its publishers, who attributed the subscriptions to Zbigniew Morsztyn. In fact, there is no reason to connect the authorship of the inscriptions with the poet, with a number of premises speaking against this hypothesis.[121] As of now, said poetic entries should thus be treated as anonymous.

The rhymed comments by an anonymous reader follow a versification scheme that is otherwise unprecedented in Polish poetry: 11(5 + 6)a, 11(5 + 6)a, 5a. Their author evidently felt at ease using it. His inspiration came from the engravings and accompanying Latin inscriptions, although he did not rely on the subscriptions of the original edition. This decision turned out to be a

---

119 Grzegorz Trościński, "*Icones mortis*: Emblematy Georgiusa Aemiliusa i Hansa Holbeina w nieznanym polskim przekazie z XVIII wieku: Z dziejów toposu tańca śmierci w Polsce," *Bibliotekarz podlaski* 27, no. 2 (2013): 51–103; Janusz and Paulina Pelc, eds., *Emblematy miłosne (Emblemata amatoria) Jacoba Catsa w trzech różnych językach, a także w ujęciu polskim z XVII wieku przedstawione* (Warsaw: Neriton, 1999); Roman Pollak, "Emblematy Anonima z początków XVII w.," in *Miscellanea staropolskie*, ed. Roman Pollak (Wrocław: Zakład Narodowy im. Ossolińskich, 1966), 2:110–31; Grześkowiak and Niedźwiedź, *Wstęp*, 335.

120 Janusz and Paulina Pelc, eds., *"Miłości Boskiej i ludzkiej skutki różne" wraz z siedemnastowieczną polską wersją tekstów do* Amoris Divini et humani effectus varii (Warsaw: Neriton, 2000).

121 Krzysztof Mrowcewicz, review of *Miłości Boskiej, Barok* 7, no. 2 (2000): 263–65; Grześkowiak and Niedźwiedź, *Wstęp*, 63.

fortuitous one, as the Polish three-verse poems often seem more interesting than the French couplets.

Michael Snijders's (*c.*1588–*c.*1630) 1626 edition contains thirty-nine numbered emblems accompanied by subscriptions. However, several of the print's surviving copies have a dozen or so (or over twenty) co-bound sheets with additional emblems.[122] Similarly, the Uppsala copy was supplemented with thirteen pages of copperplate prints. Among them were copies of two engravings from the 1627 volume *Typus mundi* (nos. 22 and 31), eight from *Amoris divini et humani antipathia* of 1628 (nos. 40, 42–48), and three more from *Amoris divini et humani antipathia sive effectus varii* of 1629 (I, 40, II, 24, 29). These sheets were apparently attached to the copies remaining in the printing house's storeroom after 1629. One of the additional cards is a copy of the engraving of the preliminary emblem from *Pia desideria*, which is why the Uppsala copy also includes a Polish subscription to said engraving.

In the copperplate, the original couplet drew the reader's attention to the heavens, inclined to hearken to the Soul's requests ("Le Ciel escoute et voit mes voeux / allez donc mes souspirs aux cyeux" [Heaven hears and sees my desires, so my sighs go to the skies]), while the anonymous subscription focuses on the praying Soul: "Chociaj z wargami język odpoczywa, / Jednak z cięciwy serca żądz się żywa / Strzałka wyrywa" (Although the tongue and the lips are at rest [silent], the heart's bowstring releases the swift arrow of desire).

The short three-verse form chosen by the anonymous author did not allow for a detailed description of the scene depicted in the engraving, or its precise interpretation and deeper reflection, for that matter. His subscriptions constitute mere lyrical sketches, albeit strikingly astute despite their laconic nature. This is also the case here. The rhyming commentary emphasizes the fervor of the prayer that is born in the supplicant's heart, as well as its meditative nature. A similar interpretation is also included in the conclusion of Mieleszko's adaptation.

3.4   *Subscriptions in Loose Engravings*

In order to reach the public, emblematic engravings did not need the medium of a book. Loose copperplate prints, sometimes combined into larger series, were equally popular at the time. One such series was signed by Cornelis Galle. The name and profession were passed down across three generations of the Antwerp Galle family: the father, the son, and the grandson, but in this case

---

122   A bibliography of French emblematic prints mentions copies with fourteen, nineteen, and twenty-one additional engravings (F.075).

we are likely dealing with Cornelis Galle II (1615–78), who was engaged in the profitable production of devotional prints. The protagonists of his series are *Amor Divinus* and the Soul in love; the cycle comprises horizontally oriented prints of similar size (43–46 × 60–63 mm) and style, derived from the images of three emblem books: van Veen's *Amoris Divini emblemata* (6, 8, 13, 21, 24, 25, 30, 33, 38, 39, 43, 46, 51, 53, 54); *Amorum emblemata*, also by van Veen (23, 93); and *Pia desideria* (I, 10, II, 5, 12, III, 2, 3).

The analysis is based on twenty-two prints (some in several copies) kept at the Ethnographic Museum in Kraków,[123] even though the cycle must have been composed of more elements. The library of the Discalced Carmelite convent in the Wesoła district in Kraków holds a copy of Bolswert's engraving for the *Pia desideria* emblem I, 2, whose format, vertical orientation, and signature "C.G." correspond to the rest of Galle's copperplate engravings, which proves that the prints preserved in the museum are not a complete series. They are part of a valuable collection of nearly fifteen hundred engravings purchased from the administrator of the congregation of the Carmelite Sisters of the Child Jesus and the confessor of the Discalced Carmelite Sisters in Wesoła in Kraków, the Discalced Carmelite Fr. Władysław of the Nativity of the Blessed Virgin Mary (Mieczysław Kluz [1925–95]). Provenance notes on the graphic prints indicate that most of the engravings come from the nunnery in Wesoła.

These prints are a perfect representation of the functioning of devotional emblems (or more broadly: engravings) in a monastic environment, demonstrating that they constituted a highly regarded source of religious excitement, used on a daily basis. In the case of the Galle prints, their reception also took a literary form, as demonstrated by anonymous tetrastich subscriptions on the margins of three engravings, added in the early eighteenth century. Two of those subscriptions refer to engravings patterned after illustrations of *Amoris Divini emblemata*, while the third evokes an illustration of *Pia desideria*. The latter is a copy of the engraving to the emblem II, 5 and its inscription, which reads, "Averte oculos meos ne videant vanitatem (*Psal*[*mo*] *118*)" (Turn away my eyes that they may not behold vanity [Ps. 118:37]).

Mieleszko's poetic elaboration of said engraving focuses on the description of the scene depicted, using it as a meditative *compositio loci*. Morsztyn referred to the biblical examples suggested in Hugo's elegy. Both poets hired by Princess Radziwiłł focused on the dangers of earthly attractions, embodied by a costumed woman. Conversely, the anonymous subscription annotated

---

123   Inventory nos. 44813–19, 44821–25, 4489, 44831–36, 44838–45. See Grześkowiak and Niedźwiedź, "Unknown Polish Subscriptions," 1–29.

on the print of the engraving seems to have a different meaning: "Więc już uciekam od Świata próżności, / Pogardzam wszystkim, a z szczyrej wdzięczności / Ku Tobie, Panie, oczów moich chęci / Obracam, Ty je utwierdzaj w pamięci" (And so I flee from vanities of the World, scorning every last one of them, and turn my eager eyes with true gratitude to you, Lord, may you bolster their memory).

While Hugo and his Polish followers highlighted the message of the psalmist, here the positive aspect prevailed: one's interest in the world was challenged in order to fully surrender to God. If we assume that the author of the quatrain was a nun living behind a cloister wall, the separation from the world mentioned in the text acquires additional significance.

The poetic subscriptions added to Galle's engravings show signs of literary refinement. The woman author was well acquainted with the poetics of the genre that stretched between the description of an engraving and the interpretation of meanings suggested by the inscription, which allows one to regard her succinct lyrical comments on a par with the religious emblems of established baroque poets.

3.5   The Artistic Reception of Engravings: A Reconnaissance

Although this study focuses on the literary reception of *Pia desideria*, it is also worth noting the existence of numerous artworks across the Polish–Lithuanian state, inspired by the engravings included in the collection.[124]

Until the mid-seventeenth century, emblematic volumes and cycles of loose copperplate engravings with devotional themes were intended exclusively for intimate reading and meditation in places of seclusion (it was no coincidence that Princess Radziwiłł did not wish to share the subscriptions commissioned from her poet clientele with the world). However, the attractiveness of the engravings designed by Bolswert gave them a life of their own, independent of the book: first, thanks to distribution in the form of engravings, both those cut out of books (I shall discuss the practice later) and those distributed as separate prints (such as Cornelis Galle II's copies circulating around monasteries and nunneries, or the loose Bolswert engravings purchased to illustrate a section of the 1673 edition of Lacki's translation); second, because the emblematic engravings became an inspiration for the painting decorations of the interior

---

124   Twentieth-century research on the visual reception of *Pia desideria* was summarized in the master's thesis of Monika Bubółka (Klimowska), "Przedstawienia wzorowane na dziele emblematycznym *Pia desideria* Hermana Hugona w polskiej sztuce nowożytnej," written under the supervision of Krystyna Moisan-Jabłońska (Cardinal Stefan Wyszyński University, Warsaw, 2000).

design and furnishings that took root in Catholic and Lutheran churches in the mid-seventeenth century.

Engravings with devotional themes that promoted innovative compositional and iconographic schemes, mass-produced and reproduced in the sixteenth and seventeenth centuries, became the most important source of invention in Catholic sacral painting. They also served as models for the decor of Lutheran churches. The very same prints inspired the works of talented artists working in metropolises and local artisans working on temple decor in peripheral areas. Just as the black-and-white graphics were endowed with a different color scheme in each painting, so were their iconographic solutions integrated into new artistic contexts, thus acquiring a unique ideological significance. A notable example is the decoration of the closet in the sacristy of a church in Sandomierz. One of its panels bears a painting that shows a scene modeled on an image from *Pia desideria*, with a representation of a skeleton with an orans imprisoned in its chest (III, 8). In the original engraving, it was the Soul clad in a simple gown; in the Sandomierz sacristy, the Soul was replaced by a young man in a cassock.[125] Although the change in setting resulted from the function of the room and the paraphernalia used by the priests, it can nonetheless be considered symptomatic of the artistic reception of the engravings included in the volume.

3.5.1 Decorative Paintings Modeled on Bolswert's Engravings

The earliest known painting decoration modeled on the *Pia desideria* engravings is believed to be the set of paintings on the organ emporium of the Lutheran church in Katharinenheerd on Eiderstedt Peninsula (Schleswig-Holstein), whose creation dates to around 1635–50.[126] The earliest painting decorations inspired by these graphics on Polish soil were created at around the same time.

Six paintings modeled after Bolswert's engravings were painted between the fourth and sixth decade of the seventeenth century in the Bridgettine

---

125 Bożena Noworyta-Kuklińska, "Program ideowy malowideł zakrystii kościoła pw. Nawrócenia świętego Pawła Apostoła w Sandomierzu," in *Fides imaginem quaerens: Studia ofiarowane Księdzu Profesorowi Ryszardowi Knapińskiemu w siedemdziesiątą rocznicę urodzin*, ed. Aneta Kramiszewska (Lublin: Werset, 2011), 151–70, here 154–56.

126 See Wolfgang J. Müller, "Die Emporenbilder von Katharinenheerd: Ein Beitrag zur Bildwelt des 17. Jahrhunderts in Schleswig-Holstein," *Nordelbingen* 40 (1971): 91–109; Ingrid Höpel, "Antwerpen auf Eiderstedt: Ein Emblemzyklus nach Hermann Hugos *Pia Desideria* in St. Katharina, Katharinenheerd auf Eiderstedt, zwischen 1635 und 1650," *De zeventiende eeuw* 20 (2004): 322–42; Höpel, "Change of Medium: From Book Graphics to Art in Sacred Space; With the Example of an Emblem-Cycle on a Church Gallery at Katharinenheerd," in *Das Emblem im Widerspiel von Intermedialität und Synmedialität*, ed. Johannes Köhler and Wolfgang Christian Schneider (Hildesheim: Georg Olms, 2007), 189–225.

church in Lublin (Church of the Assumption of the Blessed Virgin Mary of Victory). The decorations were crafted at the behest of the vigorous abbess Dorota Firlejówna (d.1660), who headed the congregation from 1632 until 1660. Paintings on wood were modeled on the engravings to the emblems 0, II, 13, III, 7, 9, 11, 13. They originally adorned the stall of novices in the side chapel, which explains why the set lacks references to the emblems from the first book of the collection, addressed to those just trying to break with their sinful nature. The images are now placed on the front of two pews in the nave. Omitted in the paintings were Latin inscriptions and irrelevant background figures or landscape elements located on the original engravings.[127]

Dating from 1671 is the confessional from the Church of the Assumption of the Blessed Virgin Mary in Nowy Wiśnicz. Two of the four paintings that adorn it are modeled on the images of *Pia desideria* 1, 6 and 8. Here, too, the painter elected to omit the inscriptions. The paintings faithfully replicate Bolswert's drawing, so much so that it can be assumed with a high degree of probability that they were patterned after the first print of the collection, two copies of which were kept in the collection of the Discalced Carmelites' monastery in Nowy Wiśnicz.[128]

In 1710, the parish priest Jakub Orzechowski (*fl.* 1706–24) sponsored the wainscot and closet for the sacristy of the Church of the Conversion of St. Paul the Apostle in Sandomierz. The Italian artist Carlo de Prevo (*c.*1670–1737), or a contractor from his workshop, decorated them with images of St. Peter, St. Paul, Christ, scenes modeled on engravings from van Haeften's *Schola cordis* volume, as well as a scene inspired by the *Pia desideria* graphic (III, 8), accompanied by the Latin inscription, "Quis me liberabit de corpore mortis?" (Who shall deliver me from the body of this death?, Rom. 7:24; fig. 5). The paintings decorating the two confessionals in the church, also linked to Prevo's workshop, date from the early eighteenth century. Four of the oil paintings are modeled on engravings from the collections *Schola cordis* (14) and *Pia desideria* (I, 8, 10 and II, 6), selected for their association with the sacrament of penance and the Savior's purifying sacrifice.[129]

---

127   Lidia Kwiatkowska-Frejlich, *Funkcje potrydenckiej sztuki kościelnej: Nowożytny wystrój kościoła Brygidek w Lublinie* (Lublin: Wydawnictwo UMCS, 2009), 191–202.

128   Maria Marcinowska, "Lubomirscy z linii wiśnickiej jako propagatorzy kultury w swoich włościach," *Zeszyty sądecko-spiskie* 3 (2008): 124–30, here 127–29.

129   Noworyta-Kuklińska, "Program ideowy," 151–70; Stanisław Gurba, "Treści przedstawień emblematycznych na konfesjonałach w kościele św. Pawła w Sandomierzu," *Kronika diecezji sandomierskiej* 107, nos. 3/4 (2014): 243–51.

FIGURE 5   Carlo de Prevo (?), painting on the wardrobe door in the sacristy of
the Church of the Conversion of St. Paul the Apostle in Sandomierz,
late seventeenth/early eighteenth century
PHOTO BY BOGUSŁAW KWIECIŃSKI

The paintings decorating the parapet of the music choir at the Church of St. Catherine of Alexandria in Nowy Targ were created before 1727. Based on Bolswert's engravings (o, I, 3, 4, 9, 10, II, 5, 14), the depictions fill seven of the nine quarters (fig. 6).[130] At one time, the starost of Nowy Targ was Jan Wielopolski (1630–88), husband of Konstancja Krystyna née Komorowska (1646–75), to whom Lacki dedicated the first print of his translation of *Pobożne pragnienia*. The painter used a copy of this edition supplied with prints of Bolswert's original copperplates imported from Antwerp, as demonstrated by the inscription accompanying the paintings. Not only is its wording consistent with Lacki's translation but the lettering was also modeled on the fonts of the printing house in Kraków that published his translation of *Pia desideria*.[131]

The appearance of fourteen paintings decorating two stalls in the presbytery and the stall in St. Joseph's chapel is linked to the changes in the decoration of the parish Church of St. John the Baptist and St. John the Evangelist in Pilica, sponsored by the local parish priest Antoni Franciszek Dunin-Kozicki (*fl.* 1765–91) in 1776. The unknown author modeled his paintings on the engravings of emblems I, 3, 8, 10, II, 5, 6, 8, 15, III, 1–3, 9–11, 13, also accounting for their Latin inscriptions (fig. 7).[132]

Also dating from the second half of the eighteenth century is the decoration of the choir parapet in St. Nicholas' Church in Kowalewo Pomorskie near Toruń. In addition to depictions of the Immaculata and personifications of Faith, Eternity, and the World (Vanitas?), the parapet features six paintings modeled on Bolswert's engravings (I, 7, III, 6, 7, 11, 12, 14; fig. 8). The painter omitted the inscriptions and slightly modified some of the iconographic patterns.[133]

---

130   Andrzej Skorupa, "*Pobożne pragnienia*: O obrazach z Frydmana i Nowego Targu," *Wierchy* 69 (2003): 166–72, here 169–72; Rafał Monita and Andrzej Skorupa, *Nowy Targ: Kościół świętej Katarzyny Aleksandryjskiej* (Kraków: Astraia 2012), 49–55.

131   Radosław Grześkowiak, "'Zwyczajem kawalerów ziemskich postępuje z nią Oblubieniec': Pierwotna dedykacja *Pobożnych pragnień* Aleksandra Teodora Lackiego jako autorski projekt lektury emblematów Hermana Hugona," *Pamiętnik literacki* 106, no. 1 (2015): 199–227, here 199–200.

132   Jan Wiśniewski, *Historyczny opis kościołów, miast, zabytków i pamiątek w olkuskiem* (Mariówka Opoczyńska: Szkoła rzemieślnicza, 1933), 292–317.

133   Polish literature on the subject is not devoid of misidentifications of engravings of *Pia desideria* as an iconographic source of sacral decorative paintings. For instance, it is not true that the decorations of stalls at the Benedictine abbey in Staniątki are modeled on engravings from Hugo's collection (Tadeusz Chrzanowski, "Kościół w Starym Mieście pod Dzierzgoniem p.w. św. Apostołów Piotra i Pawła: Emblematyka w służbie protestantyzmu," in *Sztuka Prus XIII–XVIII w.*, ed. Agnieszka Bojarska [Toruń: Wydawnictwo UMK, 1994], 199–226, here 214). In fact, they are patterned after one engraving from the volume *Schola cordis* (36), three from *Amoris Divini et humani effectus varii* (1626: 31, 33, 42), and three from *Amoris Divini et humani antipathia* by Ludovicus van Leuven (1629: 12,

Odwroć oczy moie, ábÿ niewidziáłÿ márnośći.
W Psal. 118.

Anonymous, painting on the windowsill of the music choir in the Church of
              St. Catherine's in Nowy Targ, early eighteenth century
              PHOTO BY JAKUB NIEDŹWIEDŹ

3.5.2   Decorative Paintings Modeled after an Adaptation of Engravings
           from 1628

Another set of engravings, which first adorned van Haestens's 1628 edition
and was later copied many times, also inspired paintings in the Polish–
Lithuanian state.

Said collection of engravings was used by the author of the polychromes
adorning the walls of the chamber of a manor house in Rdzawa (currently in the

---

23, 26; see Monika Anna Klimowska, "Graficzne pierwowzory alegorycznych obrazów z
opactwa sióstr benedyktynek w Staniątkach," in *Inspiracje grafiką europejską w sztuce polskiej: Czasy nowożytne*, ed. Krystyna Moisan-Jabłońska and Katarzyna Potińska [Warsaw:
Wydawnictwo UKSW, 2010], 129–44). It is also not true that the four depictions on the
polychrome at the Church of St. Stanislaus the Bishop and Martyr in Wschowa—two
in the northern nave and two in the southern nave—are modeled on engravings from
Pia desideria (Marta Małkus, "Malowane medytacje religijne inspirowane *Pia desideria*
Hermana Hugo: Program ikonograficzny polichromii w kościele pw. św. Stanisława
Biskupa i Męczennika oraz Wniebowzięcia NMP we Wschowie," in *Życie duchowe na ziemi
wschowskiej i pograniczu wielkopolsko-śląskim*, ed. Marta Małkus and Kamila Szymańska
[Wschowa: Czas A.R.T., 2017], 241–59). In fact, they are modeled on engravings from
Schola cordis (17, 20, 37, 38).

FIGURE 7   Anonymous, painting on the back of a stall in the Church of St. John the
            Baptist and St. John the Evangelist in Pilica, 1776
            PHOTO BY JAKUB NIEDŹWIEDŹ

open-air museum in Nowy Sącz). Since the monastery of the Canons Regular in the nearby Trzciana was burned to the ground and its householders murdered in the turmoil of war in the mid-seventeenth century, a new convent arrived from Kraków. As the canons, who were rebuilding the church and monastery, had to live somewhere, nobleman Stanisław Baranowski (*fl. c.*1655) made his wooden manor house available to clerics. The monks occupied it until 1703. At that time, one of the rooms was decorated with sixteen emblematic scenes taken from the *Pia desideria* volume (I, 1, 6, 8–12, 14, II, 4, 5, 7, 11–15), each of which included both the original Latin inscription and van Haestens's radically abbreviated exegetical quotation, which served as a subscription on the polychromes.[134]

The same version of the engravings was used in the mid-eighteenth century by an artisan who decorated the door of the baptismal cabinet at St. Nicholas' Church in Rychwałd with a painting based on the relevant emblem I, 8.[135]

3.5.3 Decorative Paintings in Neighboring Countries

As a context for the analysis of Catholic examples from the lands of the Polish–Lithuanian Commonwealth, it is worth mentioning analogous decorative paintings created in the Duchies of Pomerania, Prussia, and Silesia (then part of the Kingdom of Bohemia), especially since most of them are currently situated within the Polish borders.

Silesian adaptations of *Pia desideria*, which were penned by Wenzel Scherffer von Scherffenstein (1603–74; J.724/G.532), Johannes Gottfried Hoffmann (*fl.* 1666–89; J.726), and the Jesuit Georg Franz Friebel of Świdnica (1614–94; J.712), respectively, are a testament to the vibrant reception of Hugo's emblem book in the region. It was not limited to publications. After 1697, one of the most gifted painters of the Silesian Counter-Reformation, Michael Leopold Willmann (1630–1706), painted the pictures decorating the vault of the Grand Hall at the palace of Lubiąż abbots in Moczydlnica Klasztorna (Mönchmotschelnitz). Among them were four tempera paintings on wood, inspired by the engravings from a German version of *Pia desideria*: II, 1, 7, 14, III, 3.[136]

---

134 Maria Marcinowska, "Emblematy ze ścian dworu z Rdzawy w Sądeckim Parku Etnograficznym," *Rocznik sądecki* 37 (2009): 161–81.

135 Aleksander Stankiewicz, "Sanktuarium Matki Bożej Rychwałdzkiej: Na pograniczu tradycji kultu i odniesień do przeszłości w sztuce," in *Historyzm—tradycjonalizm—archaizacja: Studia z dziejów świadomości historycznej w średniowieczu i okresie nowożytnym*, ed. Marek Walczak (Kraków: Societas Vistulana, 2015), 234–48, here 246–47.

136 Andrzej Kozieł, "Willmann i barbarzyńcy, czyli słów kilka o dekoracji malarskiej stropów z dawnego pałacu opatów lubiąskich w Moczydlnicy Klasztornej," in *Opactwo cystersów w Lubiążu i artyści*, ed. Andrzej Kozieł (Wrocław: Wydawnictwo UWr, 2008), 294–310.

FIGURE 8   Anonymous, painting on the windowsill of the music choir in the Church of
St. Nicholas in Kowalewo Pomorskie near Toruń, early eighteenth century
PHOTO BY RADOSŁAW GRZEŚKOWIAK

FIGURE 9   Anonymous, painting on the frontispiece of a bench in the Church of Saints Peter
            and Paul in Stare Miasto near Dzierzgoń, late seventeenth century
            PHOTO BY KAROLINA GRZEŚKOWIAK

At the turn of the seventeenth and eighteenth centuries, at the behest
of Baron Heinrich von Zahradeck (d.1693), the former Evangelical church
(present-day Catholic Church of the Sacred Heart of Jesus) in Kościelec
(Hochkirch) near Legnica was decorated with fourteen paintings inspired by
engravings from the second and third books of *Pia desideria* (0, 11, 2, 3, 6, 8,

12, 13, III, 2–5, 9, 11, 12), which were placed on the parapet of the founders' lodge. Only some of them have survived.[137] The stylistic differences prove that the cycle was a work of two different artists, and that they were modeled not so much on Bolswert's original engravings but on a second anonymous set of copperplate engravings, processed with a degree of artistic freedom. The paintings were complemented with biblical inscriptions in German.

Similarly, the sacristy door of the former Protestant church in Przerzeczyn Zdrój (Bad Dirsdorf) is adorned with two early eighteenth-century paintings modeled on the *Pia desideria* engravings (I, 4, 10).

Also located in the former Duchy of Prussia is the richest set of decorative paintings preserved within the borders of present-day Poland. In the years 1684–88, the former Lutheran church (present-day Catholic Church of St. Peter and Paul) in the Stare Miasto (Altstadt) near Dzierzgoń was decorated with paintings by Gottfried Haarhausen (*fl.* 1684–98), who referred to himself as "a painter of courtly and hunting scenes." Haarhausen was probably also the author of the scenes copied from the *Pia desideria*, which are placed on the backrests and breastwork of the pews. Twenty-one painted panels have survived (I, 1–3, 5–7, 11–14, II, 3, 4, 7, 10, 12, 14, III, 5, 6, 12–14; fig. 9), with archival photographs proving that there were eight more (II, 13, 15, III, 3, 4, 8–11), while inscriptions over torn-out panels suggest the existence of another five (I, 8, 11, 8, III, 1, 2, 7). Modeled on the engravings from Hugo's emblem book, the rich decoration of the Lutheran church in Stare Miasto, funded by Calvinist Johann Ernst von Wallenrodt (1615–97), is an excellent example of the ease with which Hugo's volume penetrated denominational boundaries. According to the message of the elogium on the plaque in honor of the temple's founder, the images there were meant to aid earthly pilgrims in pious meditation and repayment of debt they owed to the Creator.[138]

Also interesting is the ceiling polychromes from the church in Gvardeyskoye (Mühlhausen) in former Prussia (present-day Russian Federation), commissioned by a member of the Kalkstein family and executed between 1693 and 1696 by Gottfried Hintz of Königsberg (*fl.* 1693–98). In addition to the two central paintings (III, 12, 14) on both sides of the vault, Hintz painted the

---

137   Stanisław Szupieńko, "Mistyka oblubieńcza w programie dekoracji malarskiej kościoła poewangelickiego w Kościelcu koło Legnicy," in *Willmann i inni: Malarstwo, rysunek i grafika na Śląsku i w krajach ościennych w XVII i XVIII wieku*, ed. Andrzej Kozieł and Beata Lejman (Wrocław: IHS Uniwersytetu Wrocławskiego, 2002), 192–99.

138   Chrzanowski, "Kościół w Starym Mieście," 199–226; Dagmara Liliana Wójcik, "Jezuicka mistyka w protestanckim wnętrzu: Ze studiów nad programem ideowym kościoła w Starym Mieście koło Dzierzgonia," in *Sztuka i dialog wyznań w XVI i XVII wieku*, ed. Jan Harasimowicz (Warsaw: SHS, 2000), 325–36.

equivalents of six other engravings (I, 10, 11, II, 1, 2, 5, III, 9). The side paintings included biblical verses written in German and placed on phylacteries at the top of the images, while the central paintings are only provided with sigils, which point the beholder to the appropriate inscriptions: "Psal. 42" and "Psal. 84." Hintz, too, used a different version of the engravings, which was a derivative of van Haestens's 1628 reprint.[139]

The *Pia desideria* engravings were often used as an iconographic template for decorating churches in the areas of the Lutheran Duchy of Pomerania. Two baptismal fonts by the master woodcarver Martin Edleber (*fl.* 1678–82) of Kołobrzeg (Kolberg) have survived, in which he copied prints from Hugo's volume, among other designs. The 1682 baptismal font from Konarzewo (Wachholzhagen) contains depictions patterned after images I, 10, II, 5, III, 11, as well as an adaptation of scenes II, 9 and III, 12. Similarly, the baptismal font from Otok (Woedtke), crafted at a later date, contains scenes from engravings I, 10, II, 3, 5, III, 12.[140] Also, the 1696 confessional in Wierzbno (Werben), signed "G. Pasche," is decorated with images from Hugo's emblems I, 4, 11, III, 6.[141] Four representations, II, 3, 13, III, 3, 5, can be found in the pulpit from Ostrowiec (Wusterwitz), which dates back to around 1700.[142] The richly decorated bench from Kołobrzeg (Kolberg) cathedral, crafted in 1709, contained many more such images. Only a portion can be identified in pre-war photographs, including I, 12, II, 9, 12, III, 2, 3, 5, 9, 13, 15. The artisan replaced the original inscriptions with sigils of the respective quotations, complementing each with a two-line rhymed subscription.[143] Last but not least, the iconographic program of the confessional from Jarszewo (Jassow) was decorated with a scene modeled on image of the emblem I, 9.[144]

Also located in present-day Poland is the village of Frydman, which was part of Hungary back in the seventeenth and eighteenth centuries. It was here that

139   Marcin Wisłocki, "Hugo wędruje na wschód: Uwagi o recepcji *Pia desideria* Hermana Hugona w sztuce protestanckiej Europy Środkowej," *Quart* 15, no. 2 (2020): 17–33, here 23–24.

140   Marcin Wisłocki, *Sztuka protestancka na Pomorzu 1535–1684* (Szczecin: Muzeum Narodowe, 2005), 130–32; Wisłocki, "From Emblem Books to Ecclesiastical Space: Emblems and Quasi-emblems in Protestant Churches on the Southern Coast of the Baltic Sea and Their Devotional Background," in *The Emblem in Scandinavia and the Baltic*, ed. Simon McKeown and Mara R. Wade (Glasgow: Librairie Droz, 2006), 279–84, here 280.

141   Wisłocki, *Sztuka protestancka*, 171–72.

142   Wisłocki, *Sztuka protestancka*, 257; Wisłocki, "From Emblem Books," 280.

143   Paul Hinz, *Der Kolberger Dom und seine Bildwerke: Eine Wanderung durch sechs Jahrhunderte christlicher Kunst in einer pommerschen Kirche* (Stettin: Fischer & Schmidt, 1936), 140–43; Wisłocki, "From Emblem Books," 280; Wisłocki, "Hugo wędruje na wschód," 29–30.

144   Wisłocki, "From Emblem Books," 280–81.

two *en grisaille* paintings, executed around 1760, found their way into the local Carmelite chapel at St. Stanislaus Church in the nineteenth century. One contains a cluster of three depictions from the first book (1, 2, 3, 9), with a shared inscription, "Facite fructus dignos poenaetentiae[!] (*Math.* 3)" (Bring forth therefore fruit worthy of penance; Matt. 3:8); the other includes three images from the third book (III, 2, 8, 11), with the inscription, "Diligamus Deum, quoniam ipse prior dilexit nos (*1. Ioan.* 4)" (Let us therefore love God, because God first hath loved us; 1 John 4:19). They were modeled on an iconographic variant known from Bolswert's original engravings. In both paintings, the scenes are accompanied by the original inscriptions; in the first one, they are additionally commented on with short subscriptions by the painter or inventor, selected from the exegetical excerpts collected by Hugo.[145]

3.6 Conclusions

Despite its cursory nature, the above presentation warrants some generalization. In the territories of the Polish–Lithuanian Commonwealth and its neighboring countries, the iconographic appeal of *Pia desideria* engravings extended for over a century. Decorations based on this template had already been popular among Catholics, but from the 1680s onwards they were also readily used by Lutherans in Pomerania, Silesia, and the Duchy of Prussia. This popularity followed from pietistic changes occurring within the Lutheran Church, which, instead of its previous doctrinal rigorism, began to emphasize the individual experience of the truths of faith and the sacraments (it was through no coincidence that Philipp Jacob Spener [1635–1705] titled his 1675 new piety manifesto *Pia desideria*). The spousal formula and affective tone of Hugo's/Bolswert's cycle proved to be an excellent signpost for the followers of both denominations.[146]

Once the scenes depicted in book engravings were translated into paintings in temples and clerical seats, the potentiality of readerly interaction with those images gave way to the opportunity for continuous inspection of the pictorial layer of the collection. The expansion of emblematic images beyond the confines of prints democratized their accessibility to a far greater extent than before.[147]

---

145 Skorupa, "*Pobożne pragnienia*," 166–69.

146 Wisłocki, "Hugo wędruje na wschód," 30–31. The presented conclusions owe much to the comments contributed by Marcin Wisłocki.

147 Michael Schilling, "Emblematik außerhalb des Buches," *Internationales Archiv für Sozialgeschichte der deutschen Literatur* 11 (1986): 149–74; Sabine Mödersheim, "The Emblem in the Context of Architecture," in *Emblem Scholarship: Directions and Developments;*

The division of Hugo's volume into three books, intended for penitents, those perfecting their piety, and those uniting with God, was also reflected in the use of individual scenes. Confessionals (Nowy Wiśnicz, Sandomierz, Wierzbno, Jarszewo) were most often decorated with illustrations from the first book. Emblems from the last book were used to decorate ceilings, intended to direct the thoughts of the congregation toward transcendence (Gvardeyskoye). In turn, stalls, pews (Pilica, Stare Miasto, Kołobrzeg), and galleries (Nowy Targ, Kowalewo Pomorskie, Kościelec)—that is, the furnishings in the nearest vicinity to the faithful—were decorated with images from all three books, expanding the scope of redemptive didactics.[148]

The scenes modeled on the *Pia desideria* engravings were combined with illustrations of different provenance, forming new systems of reference. In Catholic sites, they usually appear together with related scenes from *Schola cordis* (Sandomierz, Moczydlnica Klasztorna) or with personifications (Kowalewo Pomorskie); in Protestant sites, they appear with the frontispiece of the Lutheran catechism (Konarzewo), for example.

What also evolved was the language of the inscriptions accompanying the decorative paintings. Latin versions were usually preserved in the spaces intended for the clergy (Rdzawa, Sandomierz); elsewhere, vernacular versions— also legible to women—were preferred: in Silesia, the Duchy of Prussia, and the Duchy of Pomerania, they were written in German, while in the Kingdom of Poland, they were written in Polish (Nowy Targ). At the same time, the frequent omission of inscriptions in decorations, characteristic especially of Catholic sites (Lublin, Nowy Wiśnicz, Sandomierz, Rychwałd, Kowalewo Pomorskie), attests to the independence of visual compositions. Thanks to numerous reprints and their expansion into public space in the form of church decorations, the same scenes that were inextricably linked to the verse they were intended to illustrate in emblematic engravings became independent signs, carrying a message understandable to spectators about the symbolic adventures of the Soul en route to its union with God. Thus, the engravings crafted by Bolswert and his followers became a popular primer on spiritual imagery, rising to the role of a new Paupers' Bible.

The expansion of the pictorial layer of *Pia desideria*, together with the accompanying development of the ability to read the allegorical meaning behind emblematic scenes, explains why the most precious Polish cycles of religious emblems, penned by Morsztyn and Mieleszko, follow the mold of a

---

A *Tribute to Gabriel Hornstein*, ed. Peter M. Daly (Turnhout: Brepols, 2005), 159–75; Höpel, "Change of Medium," 189–99.

148   Wisłocki, "Hugo wędruje na wschód," 22–24.

reading inspired by suggestive engravings and focused on images. The works of both poets demonstrate a well-rounded command of the art of exegesis with respect to emblems consisting only of an illustration and an underpinning biblical verse. The strategy leading to the deciphering of the symbolic layer of the visual representation was the same for the Jesuit missionary and the lay Arian. The extent to which their interpretations are divergent only proves the independence of their explications, nourished by the ubiquity of devotional emblems.

4   Translations of the *Pia desideria* Elegies

4.1   *Publicity for the Genre at Jesuit Schools*
In accordance with the recommendations laid down in the *Ratio studiorum*, adopted by the Society of Jesus in 1599, college students were to study Roman erotic elegies of the Augustan period as part of their instruction in poetics, rhetoric, and grammar. Lecturers were advised to discuss them based on the most perfect representative of the genre, Ovid's *Amores*, while also ensuring that the passages covered by students were free of indecent content.

In his textbook on poetics, a contributor to the *Ratio studiorum*, Jacobus Pontanus (Jakub Spanmüller [1542–1626]), listed refinement, gentleness, subtlety, emotional complexity, and the sublime as some of the principal qualities of the elegiac style. He also appreciated the fact that the desirable writing style was unobscured by elaborate sentences but rather adorned with pleas for mercy, complaints, exclamations, apostrophes, prosopopoeia, and short digressions.[149] Such a style, dense with striking rhetorical figures, was to be employed in covering equally engaging topics. In the lectures delivered at the college in Polotsk in the 1626/27 academic year, a foremost Jesuit poet and highly respected literary theorist, Maciej Kazimierz Sarbiewski (1595–1640), lauded Roman elegiacs' ability to render complex feelings such as love, desire, sadness, inconstancy, despair, infidelity and use them to instruct readers about the faults and mistakes, as well as the troubles and tribulations of immodest life. Hence, Roman elegies were populated with daydreams, miraculous phenomena, monologues, regrets, and metamorphoses.[150]

According to Jesuit theorists, one would struggle to find another genre that would permit a more complete representation of the emotions and anxieties

---

149   [Jakob Spanmüller], *Institutio poetica* (Cologne: Sumptibus Bernardi Gualtheri, 1605), 58–59.

150   Maciej Kazimierz Sarbiewski, *O poezji doskonałej, czyli Wergiliusz i Homer* (*De perfecta poesi, sive Vergilius et Homerus*), trans. Marian Plezia, ed. Stanisław Skimina (Wrocław: Zakład Narodowy im. Ossolińskich, 1954), 307.

attendant with love. Therefore, in the lectures taught to seminarists, Sarbiewski strove to demonstrate the beauty and value of this indecent poetry. Eventually, however, he, too, rested his case, concluding: "Naturally, immature youths should be wary of reading these writings."[151]

Tapping into the tradition of the ancient genre to depict a Christianized variant of amorous affection—passionate yet devoid of indecent associations—Hugo's elegies represented the most perfect stage of its development from the point of view of Jesuit instructors. Therefore, quotations from the *Pia desideria* subscriptions began to be included in handwritten textbooks of poetics created in the Polish–Lithuanian state as an exemplary implementation of the elegy. One such case was the textbook written in 1703 at Nowodworski College in Kraków, which featured a passage (vv. 3–6, 13–16) from the elegy of emblem III, 12 as an exemplary depiction of romantic urgency.[152] That same year, an anthology of short poetic quotations was published, intended for entertainment purposes as well as to provide the reader with topics of noble conversation and supply students with inspiration for epigrammatic works, *Sales poetici, proverbiales et iocosi ad condimentum honestae conversationis, recreationem et eruditionem simul studiosae iuventutis collecti* (Poetic, proverbial, and humorous salts collected to season respectable conversation, but also for the leisure and learning of studious youth). The collection included dozens of quotations from Hugo's elegies. No wonder, then, that selected passages from his texts gained the status of "winged words" among Polish authors.

In an elegy dedicated to lustful gaze, which draws one away from God, the following couplet was included (II, 5, vv. 23–24): "O oculi, scopuli, potius Syrtesque vocandi, / Heu, quibus allisae, tot periere rates!" (Oh, eyes that should rather be called rocks and Syrtas, oh, how many ships you have lost!).[153] The simile comparing the eyes to the treacherous bays of the Mediterranean Sea, which led so many sailors to their doom, was not lost on the readers of *Pia desideria*. It was recalled by the preacher Andrzej Chryzostom Załuski (*c.*1648–1711), who was subsequently appointed bishop of Warmia and great chancellor of the crown; he used it in a sermon delivered in 1681, in which the Soul reproaches the Body for the fact that its members serve sinful purposes.[154] In a similar vein, the Discalced Carmelite Hilarion Fałęcki (*c.*1678–1756) incorporated said couplet into his enumeration of measures adopted by Satan to

---

151 Sarbiewski, *O poezji*, 309.
152 Manuscript kept at the Central Archives of Historical Records in Warsaw, call no. Sucha 243/294, 307–8.
153 Herman Hugo, *Pia desideria* (Antwerp: Hendrick Aertssens, 1624 [J.628/N.345]), 163.
154 Witold Ostafiński and Kazimierz Panuś, eds., *Kazania adwentowe* (Kraków: Unum, 2019), 254.

deceive people.[155] In his compendium *Nowe Ateny*, Chmielowski—whose interest in *Pia desideria* has already been mentioned—not only classified the juxtaposition: "Oculi–Scopuli" as a fanciful paronomasia but also pointed to its source: "Hugo: 'O oculi, scopuli, titulo meliore vocandi.'" Chmielowski evoked the same line when remarking that the windows of a monastery should not overlook secular buildings, "for *oculi sunt scopuli titulo meliore vocandi*, through the mirrors of the eyes many a Phaedra has crept into the hearts of men."[156] These quotations demonstrate the popularity of various *bons mots* extracted from Hugo's poetry.

4.2   *Three Translations into Polish*

Since the poetry collected in *Pia desideria* was widely regarded as a model rendition of elegies with Christian themes, it was worth bringing it closer to Polish and Lithuanian readers, all the more so since to translate the pieces recounting the journey from regret to reunion with God was not only a test of poetic skill but also a testament to the translator's piety. For this reason, it was primarily lay dignitaries who took an interest in translating Hugo's volume.

Today, there are three Polish-language translations of Hugo's elegies. Two of them—Lacki's rendition, created in the 1660s, and Żaba's translation penned seven decades later—include subscriptions to all of the collection's emblems. In addition, we also know of a Polish version of a single original elegy, created after 1673 and incorporated into a larger poetic whole by a consecrated author.

4.2.1   Aleksander Teodor Lacki's Translation: *Pobożne pragnienia* (Pious Desires)

The earliest Polish translation of the *Pia desideria* elegies was the work of the magnate Aleksander Teodor Lacki. From 1635 onward, Lacki held the honorary position of Lithuanian great deputy master of the pantry, and in 1654 he was promoted to the senatorial office of marshal of the court of Lithuania. Prior to that, he wrote poems intended for the sole use of his loved ones. Only three of Lacki's poems have been preserved in seventeenth-century so-called *silvae rerum* (forests of things; i.e., hand-written books that typically served as a family chronicle in the homes of the Polish and Lithuanian nobility), with the generic diversity of his work (a name-day greeting note to his wife; the

---

155   Hilarion Fałęcki, *Wojsko serdecznych nowo rekrutowanych na większą chwałę Boską afektów* (Poznań: Drukarnia Akademicka, 1746), 184.

156   Benedykt Chmielowski, *Nowe Ateny*, 2nd ed. (Lwów: Kolegium Jezuickie, 1754), 1:part 1, 63, 233. The same couplet was also paraphrased by the owner of the first printing of *Pia desideria*, the metropolitan of Ryazan, Stefan (Simeon) Iavorskii (1658–1722), whereby—for the purposes of a vanitative epigram included in the will—he replaced the word "oculi" with "tituli" (Walter Kroll, "*Poeta laureatus* Stefan Jaworski i emblematyka," *Terminus* 20, no. 2 [2018]: 195–253, here 216–18, 241–42).

praise of summer; and a propagandistic political piece) a testament to the ad hoc nature of Lacki's oeuvre, as it is to his poetic prowess. Lacki only became known to a broader literary audience with the translation of Hugo's elegies.

The full title of the first printing indicates the Latin edition that served as the basis for the Polish translation, as it contains an annotation concerning the composition of the collection: *Pobożne pragnienia trzema księgami* [...] *łacińskim opisane językiem:* 1. *Jęczenia Dusze pokutującej*, 2. *Żądze Dusze świętej*, 3. *Wdychania Dusze kochającej* (Pious desires, written in Latin in three books: 1. The groans of the penitent soul, 2. The wishes of the holy soul, 3. The sighs of the loving soul). The idea of placing the volume's synopsis on the title page was not of Lacki's making; rather, it was a translation of the information that first appeared on the frontispiece of the original in a reissue published by the Antwerp printing house of Lucas de Potter (*c.*1632–81), likely in 1657: *Pia desideria tribus libris comprehensa*: 1. *Gemitus Animae p[o]enitentis*; 2. *Vota Animae sanctae*; 3. *Suspiria Animae amantis* (J.648/N.350). This innovation in the title was quickly adopted, not least thanks to the successive printers of the volume (in the seventeenth century, the formula was repeated in the Antwerp edition of 1676 [J.654/N.354], London edition of 1677 [J.655], and the Cologne editions of 1682 [J.657] and 1694), as well as its translators, especially into German (as was the case with the 1662 adaptation by the Silesian poet Wenzel Scherffer von Scherffenstein [*c.*1603–74] [J.724/G.532] and Erasmus Finx's [1627–94] 1668 modification [J.719/G.285]) and French (Pierre de Bats's [fl. 1669–1730] edition, likely printed in 1672 [J.703], as well as the anonymous translation of 1684 [J.700/F.340]). Considering that among the Latin editions the information is only repeated on the title page of the 1676 reissue, Lacki's translation was probably based on the Antwerp edition of 1657.

Given that, in the initial 1671 preface, Lacki stated that his translation had been written some time before, one must conclude that he drafted it in the 1660s.

Planning to print the translation shortly after the nobles elected Michał Korybut Wiśniowiecki (1640–73) king of the Polish-Lithuanian Commonwealth (r.1669–73) in 1669, Lacki thought he would best serve the work by dedicating it to the monarch's mother, Gryzelda Konstancja Wiśniowiecka née Zamoyska (1623–72). These plans did not come to fruition; however, thanks to a fortunate coincidence, a manuscript copy of the draft preface from 1671 has survived.[157]

---

157   Manuscript kept by the Library of the Ossoliński National Institute in Wrocław, call no. 336/ II, 97–100. See Radosław Grześkowiak, "'Zwyczajem kawalerów ziemskich postępuje z nią Oblubieniec': Pierwotna dedykacja *Pobożnych pragnień* Aleksandra Teodora Lackiego jako autorski projekt lektury emblematów Hermana Hugona," *Pamiętnik literacki* 106, no. 1 (2015): 199–227, here 219–26.

Said dedication is a unique document when considered in the context of
the Polish reception of Hugo's volume. The author neatly transformed the
scenes and inscriptions inserted in the engravings into a personal statement
on the interpretation of the main idea of the volume. The style of the preface
imitates the occasional speeches popular among the nobility: Lacki employs
scholarly erudition, recalls miraculous events, endowing them with hiero-
glyphic symbolism, and weaves Latin interjections into the Polish language,
from single words to complete verses of the Vulgate. Such literary measures in
the dedication resulted from choosing Princess Wiśniowiecka as its addressee,
since—back in her youth—Gryzelda received her education from the finest
teachers at the Zamość Academy and was well versed in Latin.

The content of the preface breaks into two parts, with the first dealing with
the composition of Hugo's volume and the need for its translation, while the
second concerns the addressee, that is, the mother of the newly crowned Polish
monarch. In the first part, Lacki used a selection of engravings from Hugo's
collection to devise an original romance plot, played out between the Soul and
her mystical lover, with Latin inscriptions acting as statements by the female
personification of the Soul.

The description begins with the image of the enamored Soul, who, longing
for her Bridegroom, sighs a quote from the inscription to the opening emblem
of the collection (Ps. 37:10). Although the Soul yearns to take a pilgrimage to
the port of salvation, the beginning of her journey is hindered by the fact that
her beloved is missing. In the vein of emblem II, 11, the heroine searches for his
love at night. Hugo reprises an analogous scene at the beginning of the next
subscription (II, 12), where the tension is relieved by the Soul's joy at finding
the Bridegroom; however, in Lacki's work the mystical lover remains hidden,
deliberately delaying the moment of happy reunion and subjecting the lover to
a separation that takes a toll on her health:

> To test the veracity of her feelings, the Bridegroom treats her in the man-
> ner of earthly lovers. He exposes her to his various aversions, so that, hav-
> ing experienced her many tribulations, he can unveil her to the world, all
> the more magnificent at her future coronation. The Soul, whose love is
> sincere, is not discouraged in her endeavors. On the contrary, the more
> challenging the quest, the stronger the affection she lavishes on her lover.

It is only upon witnessing the Soul's steadfastness that the Bridegroom decides
to reveal himself and bring her into the Kingdom of Heaven. Lacki created a
coherent scenario along the lines of fashionable romances, in which the lovers
are separated and their love subjected to numerous trials before they are eventually reunited. At the same time, in Lacki's rendition of Hugo's collection, it

is not fate that separates the lovers but the Bridegroom himself, as he puts the Soul's affections to the test.

After outlining the vicissitudes of the amorous relationship, Lacki substantiated his decision to translate *Pia desideria*. While extolling the benefits entailed in reading Hugo's work, he remarked that Latin posed a significant obstacle for women readers, who were typically only familiar with their native language. Meanwhile, since the volume was based on a theme of bridal romance, it was precisely women who were its primary targets.

According to Lacki, the protagonist, "clad in Polish [language]" and hoping for the protection of her high-born patroness (to whom the volume was dedicated), had waited too long for the book to be published. Thus, somewhat unexpectedly, the biblical passages quoted by the Soul became an expression of a longing for the printing press:

> As she made haste to her beloved, she heaved frequent sighs to heaven, crying out, "Woe is me, that my sojourning is prolonged!" [Ps. 120:5, cf. the inscription to emblem III, 7]. Even when her fervent love prohibited further delay, she asked me if, with my permission, she could finish the journey that she had begun, "I will rise and will go about the city". [cf. Song 3:2 and inscription to emblem II, 11]

Lacki states that the woman protagonist of the collection was begotten by Hugo, raised on spiritual exercises, and enlightened by her love of God, adding that only Wiśniowiecka's patronage would enable the printing of the Polish translation of the volume. This is the lone instance throughout the extensive preface where the author demonstrates his awareness of the links between the translated collection and Ignatian meditation, crucial to the nature of Mieleszko's or Morsztyn's adaptations. More important to Lacki is the Soul's affection for her mystical Spouse and the dramatic course of their spiritual relationship. The draft of the 1671 dedication woos the reader with its brilliant use of the inscriptions from Hugo's collection and the recommended reading formula. The translator highlights the picaresque/erotic plot, advertising it to the prospective readers of the translation as a metaphysical love novella, dissected into emblematic scenes.

The manuscript copy of the original redaction of the preface is crowned with the information that it failed to be printed due to the death of her addressee. Indeed, Princess Wiśniowiecka passed away on Easter Sunday, 1672, after a short illness. Apparently, the printing was delayed, which may have been related to the efforts to procure engravings by Bolswert in order to embellish some copies of *Pobożne pragnienia*, which eventually appeared in the *in quarto* format in 1673 in the Kraków printing house run by the descendants of Krzysztof Schedel the Elder (d.1653; J.753/P.83).

The print was accompanied by a new dedication, addressed to the twenty-six-year-old Konstancja Krystyna Wielopolska née Komorowska (1647–75). Orphaned at an early age, she became the ward of her great-aunt and Lacki's future wife, Katarzyna née Komorowska (1610–75). In 1656, at the age of ten, Konstancja Krystyna was committed to the Warsaw boarding school run by the Visitandines. From 1657 to 1661, she lived with the nuns, practicing Salesian piety, learning French and reading and writing in Polish. For this reason, when composing a dedication to his wife's former ward in 1673, Konstancja Krystyna had been married for eight years to Grand Pantler of the Crown Jan Wielopolski (1630–88), Lacki prepared a text that did not contain any Latin words or expressions at all.

The new dedication contains an allusion to only a single engraving (the one that opens the collection) that depicts the Soul uttering pious sighs to God in the form of arrows:

> Since among the spiritual weapons that storm and assault the heavens, none is mightier than pious desires, which, like diamond arrows of fire, pierce the heavenly towers with their devout hardening, opening the gates of the seraphim and easing one's access to God, therefore you should rightfully own these weapons of holy desires as [they are] advantageous to your piety.[158]

For this reason, adds Lacki, although Konstancja Krystyna did not lack in similar arrows, he dared to come to her home with a ship full of *pia desideria* (pious desires), which he bestowed on her. The nautical motifs highlighted in the preface alluded to the addressee's maiden coat of arms (Korczak), which featured three rivers. Indeed, the dedication is a typical example of a laudatory text grounded in the heraldic code.

The aristocratic panegyric discourse in the Polish–Lithuanian state was strictly subordinated to heraldry, from the highly popular poems on coats of arms (*stemmata*) to the subject of occasional speeches or sermons. The ubiquitous *stemmata* were akin to the emblem, a genre that was burgeoning in the West, but since the symbolical interpretation in the former was limited to simple heraldic elements, *stemmata* remained distinctly closer to the Sarmatian imagination throughout the seventeenth century. As such, one should consider them as a hallmark of para-emblematic literary production in the Polish–Lithuanian Commonwealth.

---

158   Herman Hugo, *Pobożne pragnienia*, trans. Aleksander Teodor Lacki (Kraków: Dziedzice Krzysztofa Schedla, 1673), fol. *2ʳ.

When writing the new preface in 1673, Lacki not only dedicated the print to a different addressee; his decision to replace the romance discourse with a heraldic one implied a significant change in the nature of the text, too. The original dedication, which was a courtesy to the demands of female readers, gave way to an ennobling lecture, addressed to a representative of a magnate family.

The first printing of Lacki's work was the only illustrated edition of the Polish translation of *Pia desideria* in the seventeenth and eighteenth centuries. The Schedel printing house released part of the edition on lower-grade paper without engravings, intended for bookstore circulation. However, the other part of the said edition was issued on thicker paper and furnished with sets of forty-six sheets with prints of original copperplate engravings by Bolswert, which were imported to Kraków.

Until 1658, the original plates were a possession of the Antwerp typographer Hendrik Aertssens the Elder (1586–1658), followed by his heirs (in 1676, they were used to adorn another edition by de Potter, who was not allowed to use them during Aertssens's lifetime for the 1657 edition). Contrary to what has been written on the subject, the sons of Schedel the Elder, who were in charge of the printing press, did not import copperplate plates from Antwerp[159] but instead used sets of prints made on loose sheets of paper. They were not made to order for the Kraków printers. Sets of separate larger-format sheets containing prints of Bolswert's copperplate engravings had been available on the book market for several years. Prior to August 29, 1666, one such set was pasted into a manuscript that featured copies of Dutch translations of exegetical excerpts from Hugo's collection, among others.[160] These minuscule engravings were designed with a small-format book in mind, hence the Latin editions that they served to illustrate never exceeded the *in octavo* format. Both the Dutch manuscript and the Schedel printing house followed the *in quarto* format, and so the prints are surrounded by wide margins. In both cases, the same ready-made sets of pages with copperplate prints on thicker sheets of paper, different from that used by the Kraków printing house, were used.

Employees of the *Officina Schedeliana* pasted the prints manually into copies printed on higher-quality paper. The substantial number of these copies, preserved to this day, proves that a large portion of the edition was published

---

159   Anna Treiderowa, "Ze studiów nad ilustracją wydawnictw krakowskich w wieku XVII (z drukarń: Piotrkowczyków, Cezarych, Szedlów i Kupiszów)," *Rocznik Biblioteki Polskiej Akademii Nauk w Krakowie* 14 (1968): 5–41, here 38; Pfeiffer, "*Pobożne pragnienia*," 20; Jolanta Talbierska, *Grafika XVII wieku w Polsce: Funkcje, ośrodki, artyści, dzieła* (Warsaw: Neriton, 2011), 237.

160   Manuscript kept by Radboud Universiteit in Nijmegen, call no. 325. See Feike Dietz, "Media Literate Catholics: Seeing, Reading, and Writing in Early Modern Participatory Culture," *Authorship* 2 (2013): 1–22.

to a luxurious standard. It is therefore safe to assume that the purchase of the engravings was financed at the magnate's expense by the translator himself. The decision, however expensive, turned out to be the right one, as it significantly contributed to the dissemination of Bolswert's original engravings and the publishing success of the first edition of Lacki's translation.

The publication met with an enthusiastic reception. In the landed estates leased by Wielopolski, the release of the volume dedicated to his wife was such an important event that even years later it was noted with reverence in the chronicle of the region kept by the wójt (i.e., an official in charge of urban settlement) of Żywiec, Andrzej Komoniecki (1659–1729). In a paragraph devoted to the first printing of Lacki's translation, Komoniecki noted—not without taking due care to recall the titles and family connections between all three of the aforementioned persons—that in 1673 the husband of Katarzyna, née Komorowska, Aleksander Teodor Lacki, published a volume that he had translated from Latin "into finely chiseled and elegant Polish verse," entitled *Pobożne pragnienia Duszy pokutującej, świętej i kochającej* (Pious desires of a penitent, holy, and loving soul). Divided into three books, the work contains imported copperplate engravings and is dedicated to the heiress of Żywiec, Konstancja Krystyna Wielopolska née Komorowska.[161] Thus, Komoniecki not only admitted that he had seen one of the luxury copies stocked with engravings but was also aware that the prints had been imported from abroad specifically for said book.

The chronicler's note attests to the local interest in the print, but it also aroused the enthusiasm of the leading poet of the Polish baroque, Wespazjan Kochowski (1633–1700). Kochowski's epigrams, published in 1674 as a volume entitled *Niepróżnujące próżnowanie* (Not idling idleness), included a triptych that constituted the laudation of the edition published the year before. The first poem of the cycle, *"Pobożne pragnienia" J[aśnie] W[ielmożnego] J[ego] M[ości] p[ana] Teodora Lackiego, marszałka nad[wornego] lit[ewskiego] edycyi* (Pious desires, published by his lordship Teodor Lacki, court marshal of the Grand Duchy of Lithuania), praised the artistic quality of the translation as much as it did the importance of the volume's religious subject matter. The next epigram *Do tegoż* (To the same) contains a more ingenious compliment: Kochowski refers to Lacki's poem as "angelic," as it paves the way to the heavens, where angels have their dwelling. The high praise for Lacki's text is followed by Kochowski's laudation of the author: the virtue of a translator who writes about heaven with such enthusiasm will surely secure him an introduction to it. The final part of the triptych, entitled *Ex utroque Caesar [mundo]* (Caesar from both [worlds]), uses the well-known praise of Caesar, who was as much of a gifted leader as a talented

---

161   Andrzej Komoniecki, *Chronografia albo Dziejopis żywiecki*, ed. Stanisław Grodziski and Irena Dwornicka (Żywiec: Towarzystwo Miłośników Ziemi Żywieckiej, 1987), 223.

author, a measure that was also popular in emblematic circulation. The engraving showing the ruler wearing a crown with a sword in one hand and a book in the other was included in the emblematic collection by Gabriel Rollenhagen (1583–1619).[162] Kochowski related this representation to Lacki: he is seen holding a staff (an attribute of the marshal's office) in one hand, so as to exercise his authority, and a pen in the other, so as to practice poetry in his spare time; in both instances, he is seen as a successor of the Roman ruler.[163]

With his edition of *Pobożne pragnienia*, Lacki also earned a place in the pantheon of native poets that Kochowski outlined in his poem *Poetowie polscy świeższy i dawniejszy we dworze helikońskim odmalowani* (Past and present Polish poets painted at the court of Helicon), published as part of the same collection. Enumerating the most prominent Polish lyricists, Kochowski devoted a separate quarto to Stanisław Herakliusz Lubomirski (1642–1702) and Lacki (vv. 51–54). Kochowski considered them to be equal as poets and as senators, for Lacki had served as the court marshal of the Grand Duchy of Lithuania, while Lubomirski had been named court marshal of the crown a year earlier, hence they held parallel offices, one in the Grand Duchy of Lithuania, the other in the Kingdom of Poland.[164] The wit was founded on the equivalence of senatorial positions, which prompted Kochowski to put the talents of the two poets on a par as well. The latter comparison was clearly farfetched, for while Lubomirski was an outstanding and versatile artist of words, Lacki was merely a skilled literary craftsman.

Commending the *Pobożne pragnienia* volume published a year earlier, Kochowski contented himself with panegyric generalizations. What is important, however, is that he wrote highly of the importance of this translational endeavor and did not hesitate to publicize it.

The 1673 edition must have had a wide circulation. This is indicated both by the number of surviving copies and by the fact that the collection must have remained on sale for many years, since it was only twenty-four years after the release of the first edition that the printer decided to reprint it. The matter of reprinting was simpler at the time, since the translator had been dead for several years and there was no need to negotiate the due royalties. It also meant that someone else had to come up with the funds necessary to print the volume. According to the information on the title page, the 1697 reissue (J.755/P.84; fig. 10), published by the same Kraków printing house,

---

162 Gabriel Rollenhagen, *Nucleus emblematum selectissimorum* (Cologne: Crispijn van de Passe, 1611), 1:book 1, no. 32.

163 Wespazjan Kochowski, *Nieprόżnujące prόżnowanie* (Kraków: Wojciech Górecki, 1674), *Epigramata*, 121.

164 Kochowski, *Nieprόżnujące prόżnowanie*, *Lirica*, 320.

FIGURE 10   Anonim, frontispiece in: Herman Hugo, *Pobożne pragnienia*, trans. Aleksander
Teodor Lacki (Kraków: Mikołaj Aleksander Schedel, 1697), engraving. The
University of Warsaw Library

run by Mikołaj Aleksander Schedel (1644–1708) at the time, was financed by his brother and recent partner, the then city councilor and bookseller Jerzy Romuald (1635–1704). It was Romuald who saw to it that the reprint was published in the more convenient *in octavo* format.

The change of person financing the printing resulted in a change of approach to the layout. Prints of Bolswert's engravings were probably no longer available on the book market, and Schedel was unlikely to invest in them either. However, as a bibliopole professionally involved in the book trade, he was cognizant of how much graphic design affects the attractiveness of any publication, thereby driving up sales figures. Therefore, Schedel supplied the reissue with a copperplate frontispiece made by a local engraver patterned after the original one attributed to Bolswert. The Polish frontispiece is larger and has slightly different proportions (it is wider). Except for the abbreviations of biblical books, all Latin textual elements in the engraving—affective exclamations and questions on the wing feathers, biblical quotations next to each figure—were Polonized. The artistic quality of the copperplate engraving pales in comparison to the frontispiece of the original print but is comparable to the copies used for the Dutch reissues, such as the 1657 reissue published by Potter's Antwerp printing house (J.648/N.350).

Considering that Lacki had long been dead at the time, as had the addressee of his preface, the reprint did not include the original dedication, nor was a new one incorporated in its place. Also missing were any other elements of the publishing framework that would recommend the volume to prospective buyers.

The final reissue of Lacki's translation was published in 1737 (J.756/P.85). Although the work did live to see three editions, it was only printed twice, as a matter of fact. This is because the second reissue was an edition in which only the title page was changed in order to market as a publishing novelty a portion of the 1697 edition that had not sold out for four decades.

This type of venture suggests that one of two things happened: either the second edition sold so poorly that a large number of surplus copies was still in stock forty years after printing, or the title still found its buyers, although the volume of the second edition was significantly overestimated. I am leaning toward the second explanation. The bookseller Jerzy Romuald Schedel had a good understanding of readers' needs. He invested exclusively in lucrative reissues of popular handbooks, textbooks, and editions of the works of classics such as Cicero and Virgil. Moreover, although this was by no means a rigid rule, the more recent the edition, the more copies have typically survived;

meanwhile, the 1737 edition is known only from one unique copy.[165] This would suggest that the number of unsold copies, which comprised the run of the "new" edition, was limited. Other data also indicate that the demand for the 1697 edition must have been high. As many as three copies have survived in the book collection of the Discalced Carmelite convent in Kraków (Wesoła) alone. The high demand for printing the Polish version of *Pia desideria* is also indicated by the fact that, although Lacki's translation was available in book-stores for at least seventy years, handwritten copies of this translation can be found in household *silvae rerum* from the late seventeenth and eighteenth centuries.[166]

In order for the print that had been stuck in storage for forty years to pass as a new edition in 1737, it was necessary to replace the title page. Since the plate with the frontispiece (which would have been easy to rearrange by changing the date) had been lost in the printing house over time, the printer decided to fold the new title page in fonts, trying to preserve all textual elements. Its cen-terpiece is a heart composed of printing ornaments, with the title inscribed in the middle. Apart from the heart, the title page features the text of the excla-mations and questions that were originally embedded in the wings that lift the heart, as well as the quotations that accompanied the silhouettes of the biblical authors, all in italics. The date was changed in the publishing address, while the rest of the information was faithfully repeated after the frontispiece. The result was perhaps the crudest title page in the history of vernacular *Pia desideria* reprints (fig. 11).

The reissue of 1737 concludes the publishing history of Lacki's translation.[167]

---

165   Copy kept at the Library of the Institute of Literary Research of the Polish Academy of Sciences in Warsaw, call no. XVIII.1.146. Michal. The second copy noted in bibliographies (see J.756) of the Jagiellonian Library in Kraków, call no. 1046 I, is defective and miss-ing the title page. And since the title page is the only distinctive difference between the second and third editions of Lacki's translation, it is impossible in this case to determine whether said book is a copy of the 1737 edition.

166   Such a copy was found in a codex transcribed in 1701 in Lutsk, the capital of the former Volhynian Voivodship (manuscript kept at the Library of the Polish Academy of Arts and Sciences and the Polish Academy of Sciences in Kraków, call no. 1278, 55–60). It includes the first three emblems from Lacki's translation (the initial one and the first two from book 1), ending with the inscription of emblem I, 3.

167   Some studies incorrectly list more editions. The introduction to the contemporary edition of Lacki's translation erroneously states that it was published six times, in 1673, 1697, 1737, twice in 1744, and in 1774, respectively (Krzysztof Mrowcewicz, "Wprowadzenie do lektury," in Aleksander Teodor Lacki, *Pobożne pragnienia*, ed. Krzysztof Mrowcewicz [Warsaw: Wydawnictwo IBL, 1997], 8). The latter three phantom editions are the by-product of a build-up of several bibliographical errors and did not actually come into existence. The

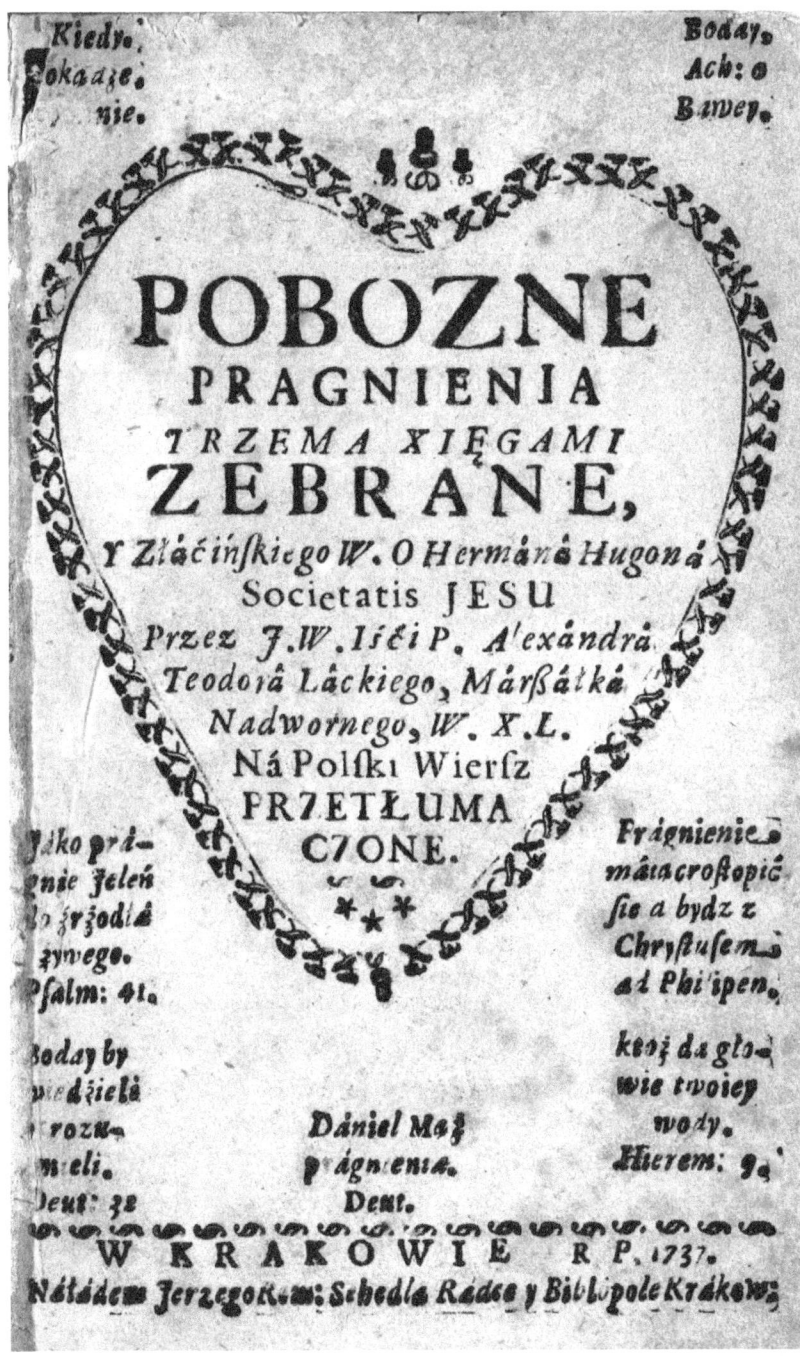

FIGURE 11   Herman Hugo, *Pobożne pragnienia*, trans. Aleksander Teodor Lacki
(Kraków: Jerzy Romuald Schedel, 1737), title page. Warsaw, Library of the
Institute of Literary Research of the Polish Academy of Sciences

4.2.2   Anonymous Translation: *Na słowa "Psalmu siedmdziesiątego*
            wtórego" przydatek (Appendix on the Words of "Psalm 72")
The convent's book collections contain copies of a manuscript emblem book
addressed to the nuns, compiled on the basis of the graphic series *Cor Iesu*
amanti sacrum, which the Jesuits commissioned from Anton II Wierix around
1600. Its central motif is the heart of a believer, providing the backdrop for the
scenes starring the Infant Jesus. The intimate religious experience is dissected
into eighteen copperplate engravings accompanied by rhymed inscriptions in
Latin, which take the form of stanzas modeled on *Stabat Mater*. The graphic
series was extremely successful. By the mid-eighteenth century, it had been
copied by over twenty different engravers, and from 1626 onward it was also
the basis of numerous literary studies, including several in Polish.[168]
    The manuscript book is anonymous, untitled, and offers no indication of
precise dating (first half of the eighteenth century?). The known copies were
transcribed by the same nun, most likely a Discalced Carmelite sister, and
since they represent different redactions of the text, said nun was most probably the work's author. The text has survived in the form of two manuscript
versions: the earlier one is part of the book collection of the Poor Clares convent in Stary Sącz, with the ownership notes of the codex indicating that it
was previously owned by the Benedictine nuns of Staniątki near Kraków;[169]

---

      alleged 1774 edition (*J.760/P.89) is an error in the bibliography of *jesuitica* (Augustin de
      Backer, Aloys de Backer, and Carlos Sommervogel, eds., *Bibliothèque des écrivains de la*
      Compagnie de Jésus [Liège: Grandmont-Donders, 1893], 4:520). The reissue of 1744 (in
      reality not one, but two) (J.757/P.86 = *J.758/P.87) is the first edition of Żaba's translation
      (see Paulina Buchwald-Pelcowa, "Typologia polskich książek emblematycznych," *Barok* 3,
      no. 1 [1996]: 59–75, here 71), rather than a reprint of Lacki's rendition. The authors of *The*
      Jesuit Series, Peter M. Daly and G. Richard Dimler, also point to another error (Backer,
      Backer, and Sommervogel, *Bibliothèque*, 520), involving the printing date of 1673 being
      listed as "1674," which led to the birth of another phantom edition of the book (*J.754).
      The Central Catalog of Early Prints of the National Library in Warsaw lists an edition
      from 1691, a copy of which was said to be kept in the library of the Discalced Carmelite
      convent in Kraków (Buchwald-Pelcowa, "Typologia polskich książek emblematycznych,"
      71); as a matter of fact, said collection only includes copies of the 1697 edition. In turn,
      Mario Praz (1896–1982) mentions a reprint of Lacki's translation, released in 1843 (Mario
      Praz, *Studies in Seventeenth-Century Imagery* [Rome: Edizioni di Storia e Letteratura,
      1974], 2:377), which actually pertains to a paraphrase by Bonifacy Ostrzykowski (J.761)
      (see Grześkowiak, "'Zwyczajem kawalerów,'" 207–8).
168   Mieleszko, *Emblematy*, 169–211, 333–52; Radosław Grześkowiak and Paul Hulsenboom,
      "Emblems from the Heart: The Reception of the *Cor Iesu amanti sacrum* Engravings
      Series in Polish and Netherlandish 17th-Century Manuscripts," *Werkwinkel* 10, no. 2 (2015):
      131–54, here 143–52.
169   Janusz Królikowski, ed., *"Serce me daję": Archiwum Klarysek w Starym Sączu 2* (Tarnów:
      Biblos, 2012).

the library of the Norbertine nuns in Imbramowice currently preserves a later, considerably expanded version. Both redactions consist of chapters based on sixteen engravings from *Cor Iesu amanti sacrum*. Each chapter begins with a pasted-in copy of an engraving by Michael Snijders (*c*.1588–*c*.1630), a Polish translation of its Latin inscription, lead quote(s) from the Bible, and a poetic subscription containing a description and interpretation of the scene depicted in the engraving. These are followed by written prose meditations, which occasionally expand into extensive treatises that absorb other literary forms and texts, including minor poetic works, among others those with an emblematic structure.[170]

The entire work is punctuated by the elaborate poem *Na słowa "Psalmu siedmdziesiątego wtórego" przydatek: "Cóż mi jest na niebie abo co będzie miała ziemia, czego bym od Ciebie pragnąć miała? Ustało ciało moje i serce moje, Boże serca mego i części moja, Boże na wieki"* (Appendix on the words of "Psalm 72": "For what have I in heaven or what will the earth have, what I would like to get from you? My flesh and my heart hath fainted away, God of my heart and my portion, God forever").[171] The bulk of the poem (vv. 1–74) constitutes a faithful and poetically effective translation of Hugo's elegy (III, 6, vv. 1–78). A notable error indicates that it is unlikely that the translation was the work of the author of the two manuscript redactions: the copy used by the nun shows a typical scribal error, suggesting that she was referring to a now-unknown translation of Hugo's elegies, made by someone else.

The poem must have been written after 1673, since the author made minor borrowings from Lacki's translation. The most striking among them is the noticeable correspondence of the first line of the couplet (vv. 45–46) "Jednak między tak wielą niebieskich światłości / Żadna nie oświecała dusze mej ciemności" (However, of so many heavenly lights, none has illuminated the darkness of my soul) with the analogous passage from the 1673 translation (vv. 41–42): "Jednak między tak wielą niebieskich światłości / Żaden ogień nie zmiękczył dusze mej chciwości" (However, of so many heavenly lights, no flame has quenched the thirst of my soul).

---

170   Radosław Grześkowiak, "Anonimowe dzieło emblematyczne na kanwie cyklu rycin *Cor Iesu amanti sacrum* Antonia Wierixa z drugiej połowy XVII stulecia," *Pamiętnik literacki* 104, no. 3 (2013): 217–30.

171   As per Radosław Grześkowiak, "'Po różnych królestwach i prowincyjach Dusza nabożna szukała kochanka swego': Stratyfikacja staropolskiej recepcji jezuickich druków emblematycznych na przykładzie *Pia desideria* Hermana Hugona," in *Formowanie kultury katolickiej w dobie potrydenckiej*, ed. Justyna Dąbkowska-Kujko (Warsaw: Wydawnictwo UW, 2016), 249–99, here 295–99.

Since this influence is limited to a handful of rhyming pairs, the high degree of independence from the work of its predecessor shows the independence of the translation. On the other hand, the translator's knowledge of Lacki's work does have a chronological value, as it suggests that the anonymous translation must have been written after 1673.

In *Pia desideria*, the inscription in emblem III, 6 is a rhetorical question (Ps. 72:25). The nun complemented it with the next verse of the very same psalm (Ps. 72:26), which makes a reference to the heart of God's servant, to whom her entire emblematic volume was dedicated. The nun adopted the poetic reflection on the first verse from the anonymous translation of Hugo's poem, while adding the next forty-four verses of her own, in which she elaborated on the leading theme of the second verse. The compilation seemingly constitutes a coherent whole, largely thanks to the deliberate efforts of the gifted nun. Whenever the Antwerp Jesuit mentions satiation or contentment, the nun's version makes a reference to the heart (a total of eleven lines were altered this way), referencing it fourteen more times in the verses of her own. These repetitions were in close correlation with the cordial theme of the work that concluded with this poem, and as such they account for the minor modifications to the earlier translation.

Apart from the redrafting of one elegy, no other traces of this translation are known as of today; therefore, it is impossible to determine whether it was limited to a single poem or constituted a complete translation of all of Hugo's elegies.

4.2.3   Jan Kazimierz Żaba's Translation *Pobożne żądania* (Pious
          Demands)
The interest in *Pia desideria*, especially in the eastern borderlands of the Polish–Lithuanian state, did not wane in the first half of the eighteenth century. At the time, another senator, voivod of Minsk, Jan Kazimierz Żaba, undertook a new translation on account of the fact that several decades had passed since Lacki's translation, whose Polish had by then become old-fashioned (the translators were divided by a gap spanning two generations).

Żaba was one of the three sons of the vice-palatinus of the Polotsk Voivodship and colonel in a hussar regiment, Hieronim Żaba, and Katarzyna née Protasiewicz. Jan Kazimierz followed in his father's footsteps, serving as a hussar colonel and regiment commander in the Lithuanian army. The local nobles held him in high esteem, repeatedly electing him deputy to the tribunals and deputy to the Sejm. In 1721, he was appointed voivod of Minsk and was the first of his line to be named senator. Before 1709, he married the daughter of the standard-bearer of Lviv, Barbara Ludwika Dzieduszycka, with whom he had two daughters and five sons. Jan Kazimierz died at the age of seventy-one.[172]

The Żabas were known for their piety. In 1716, Hieronim and his wife brought the Dominican monks to the family estate of Ushachy (present-day Belarus), sponsoring a monastery and church, and bequeathing 1,500 thalers for their upkeep. Jan Kazimierz increased this fund. In July 1757, after his passing, his son Franciszek (b. *c*.1720) and his daughter-in-law Cecylia (née Lipska, b. *c*.1720) formally established the first branch of the Brotherhood of the Heart of Jesus in Lithuania, also sponsoring a painting with the Sacred Heart, richly decorated with Cecylia's jewels, for the Basilian church in Ushachy. The fervent religiosity instilled in Jan Kazimierz by his parents is also demonstrated by the fact that three of his five sons entered religious orders: Stanisław (1710–74; Jesuit since 1727) Ignacy (1713–80; Jesuit since 1729), and Dionizy (joined the Basilian order). After years of service in Jesuit education, Stanisław was named rector of the Vilnius Academy, while Ignacy was appointed rector of the Jesuit colleges in Vitebsk, Grodno, Zhodishki (present-day Belarus), and Kražiai (present-day Lithuania).

Literary talents were not unusual in the Żaba family. Poetics and rhetoric were taught at Jesuit colleges by Jan's sons, Ignacy and Stanisław, with the former trying his hand at poetry and the latter establishing himself as a sermon writer. The sons must have learned literary culture from their family home, although little is known about the poetic works of the voivod of Minsk. Apart from the translation of *Pia desideria*, he was the author of the rhymed *Historia męki Pańskiej* (History of Lord's passion), which was not published. It is significant that when the Jesuit Kazimierz Świrski (1688–1750) dedicated his panegyric epigram to Żaba in 1749, he praised Jan exclusively on account of his military exploits.[173] Apparently, Żaba's contemporaries also knew little of his affinity for poetry.

The decision to undertake a new translation of the *Pia desideria* elegies was not driven by Żaba's literary ambition but his religious motivations. Żaba regarded his translation as godly work performed for the greater glory of God. The formula *Ad maiorem Dei gloriam* at the end of the translation appears in both editions published by different printing houses, which indicates that it was added by the author. This is also demonstrated by the fact that, although Żaba worked on the translation for over a decade, he only had the

---

172   Biographical details after Teodor Żychliński, *Złota księga szlachty polskiej* (Poznań: Jarosław Leitgebr, 1881), 3:323–24.

173   Kazimierz Świrski, *Honor laureis poeticis coronatus* (Lublin: Kolegium Jezuickie, 1749), fol. C3ʳ.

text published when on his deathbed, hence it was not poetic fame that he was after but a work that would bring him closer to salvation.

The 1744 printing of the original redaction of Żaba's translation featured the following information on the title page: *Pobożne pragnienia* [...], *przedtym po łacinie przez w[ielebnego] o[jca] Hermana Hugona Soc[ietatis] Iesu, a teraz przez wielkiego senatora W[ielkiego] Ks[ięstwa] L[itewskiego] przetłumaczone, a przez jednego szlachcica z raptularza szczęściem dostanego przepisane i do druku podane* (Pious desires [...], first published in Latin by the reverend Jesuit father Herman Hugo, now translated by a distinguished senator of the Grand Duchy of Lithuania, and by a certain nobleman from a fortuitously procured rough draft copied and submitted for printing).[174] The details of said nobleman are known, as he signed the preface to the edition. The man in question was the pantler of Orsza, Jan Turczyn (*fl.* 1740s). A benefactor of the Uniate church in the village of Ballia, which he owned (and generously endowed the local Uniate priest the following year), he was likely a Uniate himself. Admitting—on the title page at that—to publish a copy of someone else's translation, which Turczyn had come across by accident, proves he had quite the nerve, all the more so given that the personal details of the actual translator were glossed over in silence. This is compounded by the fact Turczyn's mention of the translator clearly indicates that he must have known the person in question was the aged voivod of Minsk. This edition evidently appeared without the poet's knowledge or consent and was therefore unauthorized. Perhaps it was on account of these considerations that the title page only contained the year of printing, lacking any information on the place of publication and the printing house that released the book. Only a typographical analysis made it possible to establish that the book was published in the printing house of the Basilian fathers in Supraśl.[175] The circulation of this unauthorized edition was rather modest, since only two copies have survived to this day, one in Poland and the other in Lithuania.

Turczyn published the translation to ingratiate himself to his principal, Ignacy Ogiński (*c.*1698–1775), the grand camp leader of Lithuania, and his wife, Helena (1700–90), famous for her piety, sharp wit, and extraordinary physical strength (which, even at an advanced age, she would put on display by breaking horseshoes and rolling silver plates in her hands). In a short dedication, Turczyn highlights the fervent religiosity of the addressees and their

---

174 Herman Hugo, *Pobożne pragnienia* [trans. Jan Kazimierz Żaba] ([Supraśl: Drukarnia Bazylianów], 1744 [J.757/P.86 = *J.758/P.87]).
175 Maria Cubrzyńska-Leonarczyk, *Katalog druków supraskich* (Warsaw: Biblioteka Narodowa, 1996), 67.

generosity in founding churches and their furnishings, as well as their numerous deeds of charity. The dedication ends with Turczyn wishing the couple a long life, followed by the realization of their "pious desire" for salvation and heavenly ambrosia.

On the title page, the publisher confessed that the book was a copy of "a fortuitously procured rough draft." The actual translator, who was thus robbed of his work, would doubtless not dub this incident fortunate, though it was, indeed, fortuitous for those studying the reception of Hugo's work. Turczyn published a draft version of the translation, one that Żaba was still working on. As a result, we are now able to compare his two redactions of the work and learn more about the voivod of Minsk as a translator.

Even in the original redaction of the translation, one can discern the emulative efforts undertaken by Żaba, who—much like the anonymous monastic translator—worked with Lacki's edition by his side. Since the new translation was to be superior to the existing one, Żaba did his best to conceal his knowledge of Lacki's solutions. However, he did not always succeed in doing so. In some instances, Żaba repeated after Lacki the pre-caesura elements while radically changing the post-caesura ones in favor of new (and, in his view, improved) rhymes. And yet, on other occasions even he had to yield, resorting to the rhymes devised by his predecessor. These cases are common enough to attest to Żaba's thorough knowledge of the translation published in the preceding century.

The second edition of the translation was published ten years later by the Jesuit printing house in Vilnius, under a different title: *Pobożne żądania* [...], *niegdy przez wielebnego księdza Hermana Hugona Societatis Iesu łacińskim wierszem napisane* [...], *teraz zaś przez Jaśnie Wielmożnego Jegomości Pana Jana Kościeszę Żabę, wojewodę mińskiego, na polski język przełożone i do druku podane* (Pious demands [...], originally penned in Latin verse by the reverend Jesuit Priest Herman Hugo [...], presently translated into Polish by his honorable lordship voivod of Minsk, Jan Żaba of the Kościesza coat of arms, and published in print).[176] The imprimatur, issued by Aleksander Horain the Elder (d.1774), archdeacon of Vilnius and censor of books published in this city, bears the date of March 18, 1754. It is therefore doubtful that the translator, who died on May 16 of that year, lived to see the publication, but its form can be considered consistent with the author's intentions.

The translation bears no dedication. Its absence is explained by the aforementioned formula at the end of the translation, which attests that the text was

---

176   Herman Hugo, *Pobożne żądania*, trans. Jan Kościesza Żaba (Vilnius: Akademia Jezuicka, 1754 [J.759/P.88]).

intended as a work for the greater glory of God but at the same time deprives
the reader of a chance to get acquainted with a potential self-commentary
by the aged translator.

A comparison of the texts of translation in the 1744 and 1754 editions
proves that we are dealing with two significantly different redactions of the
translation. Żaba painstakingly chiseled his work. If at first, he happened to
spend four lines on the translation of an elegiac couplet, in the second edition,
he curtailed his verbosity. For example, the sentence (III, 13, vv. 1–2) "Quam
mea per varios vita est exercita casus, / Ut pila percussu pulsa repulsa manus"
(My life is affected by various misfortunes, like a ball that is hit and deflected
by a hand) was originally amplified as follows (1744: III, 13, v. 1–4): "Ach, jak
moje przez różne życie utrapienia / Wypróbowano, niby piłka z uderzenia /
Dziecinnej ręki, którą, jako chce, obraca, / Bo raz naprzód, drugi raz nazad
onę wraca!" (Ah, how my life has been tried by all sorts of misfortunes, like
a ball struck with a child's hand, which spins as he pleases, moving to and
fro!). However, after editing, the same sentence fit was reduced to a couplet:
"Jak różnemi przypadki byłam nagabana, / Jak piłka w ręku dzieci tam i sam
rzucana" (What different misfortunes have befallen me, like a ball tossed to
and fro by children's hands).

In the second redaction, the translator also improved the rhyme scheme,
reducing the enjambments, whose original profusion was typically condi-
tioned by his difficulties in finding the right rhyme. Additionally, he polished
the syntax of the respective sentences, opting for a more natural word order.
As a result of these measures, the differences between the redactions are not
limited to mere word substitutions but rather constitute reworkings of entire
passages that also extend to rhymes.

Striving to achieve more emphatic wording in the second redaction, Żaba
would deviate from the original phrasing. A notable case in point is the
embodiment of the Soul's Bridegroom. In the Latin text and, consequently, in
the initial redaction of the translation, that person is often left unspecified; in
the second redaction, Żaba readily identifies the Bridegroom with Jesus. For
example, in emblem II, 9, the Bridegroom takes the form of a two-year-old
boy ("puerum"), hence his initial denotation in the translation as "little child"
(v. 25), which was subsequently changed to: "Jesus, the child." In a similar vein,
the original wording, "I would kiss your lovely little face," was replaced by the
phrase, "Jesus, I would kiss your lovely face" (v. 64). In the Soul's utterances
addressed to the Divine Love, Hugo was fond of using apostrophes, such as
"mea lux," "mea vita"; Żaba translated some of them faithfully in both editions,
while others were subjected to significant concretization, such as the expression "mea vita" (III, 5, v. 55), translated as "my light" in the initial redaction and

"my Jesus" in the second one; or "mea lux" (III, 6, v. 5), translated as "my light" and "Jesus," respectively. After all, it was not the translator's priority to give a faithful rendition of the original but to unambiguously interpret the theological realities of the lyrical situation.

Also significant was the change of title. Żaba originally opted for Lacki's proposal. Turczyn's 1744 edition was titled *Pobożne pragnienia*; below the title itself, the title page bore the headings of the three books, which were also unanimous with the subtitles known from the title page of the first edition of Lacki's 1673 translation. Such far-reaching similarities could easily have led to the identification of the two translations and the conclusion that the edition of Żaba's redaction was not a new translation per se but rather a reissue of Lacki's translation.[177] Therefore, in the authorized edition, Żaba's translation was published under a different title: *Pobożne żądania*. The headings of the first two books remained unchanged, while the third was supplemented with a new component: instead of *Westchnienia Duszy kochającej* (The sighs of the loving soul—which was the case in Lacki's translation and in Turczyn's edition), Żaba opted for *Westchnienia Duszy kochającej Boga* (The sighs of the soul in love with God). Apparently, such a clarification of the title seemed necessary given the widespread popularity of French romances at the time.

It should be noted that Żaba's translation only lived to see two editions, the unauthorized one from 1744 and the authorized one from 1754, because—much like in the case of Lacki's rendition—errors and misunderstandings by bibliographers that have contributed to the emergence of phantom editions continue to be perpetrated even in modern-day research.[178]

As of now, the actual distribution of the two editions of Żaba's translation is difficult to establish. Turczyn's testimony proves that, even during the translator's lifetime, his work was copied and disseminated in the form of manuscripts, although no surviving copies are known today. Annotations on the

---

177   That this danger was real is best demonstrated by the kind of misattribution made by a contemporary researcher: Pfeiffer, "*Pobożne pragnienia*," 17–18; see Buchwald-Pelcowa, "Typologia polskich książek emblematycznych," 71.

178   As a result of a bibliographer's error, the 1744 edition multiplied into two different editions—(J.757/P.86) and (*J.758/P.87)—with the error still repeated today, despite being corrected in 1996 (Buchwald-Pelcowa, "Typologia polskich książek emblematycznych," 71). The phantom reissue of 1774 (*J.760/P.89) is a result of a slip-up in the old bibliography (Backer, Backer, and Sommervogel, *Bibliothèque*, 520). Similarly, the information provided by the modern-day publisher of Lacki's translation, according to whom Żaba's translation had two editions, one published in 1754, and the other after 1754 (Mrowcewicz, "Introduction," 8), is incorrect. Mrowcewicz drew it from Pfeiffer's work, which refers to editions of 1754 and 1774 (Pfeiffer, "*Pobożne pragnienia*," 18), even though the latter never came to be.

existing printed copies usually point to clerical readers. A copy of the 1744 edition was in the possession of the Jasna Góra monastery in Częstochowa, with another one added to the book collection of the Dominican novitiate in Poporcie (present-day Lithuania) in 1783.[179] In turn, a copy of the 1754 edition was owned by the Piarist parish priest of Pinsk, Antoni Moszyński (1800–93).[180]

4.2.4   Strategies Employed by the Translators of Hugo's Elegies

The following comments primarily concern Lacki's and Żaba's translations. As far as possible, I also seek to consider the anonymous translation, preserved in the form of one incomplete elegy and known only from second-hand.

All three translators adopted only two components from Hugo's emblems: elegies and biblical inscriptions. Lacki and Żaba (the latter at least initially) translated the Vulgate verses on their own. In the final redaction of Żaba's translation, each elegy was preceded by a verse in bilingual form, that is, in Latin and Polish, based on Wujek's translation of the scriptures. Similarly, the anonymous nun translator who quoted two biblical verses in the title of the work used Wujek's translation as a reference.

The translators translated the elegies using the Polish alexandrine (7 + 6) rhyme scheme, popular in Polish poetry. A number of common stylistic solutions have a school provenance. This is especially true of the principle that each couplet of the original should be rendered in two lines, a principle that, even if not without exceptions, applied to all three translators. When Polonizing Latin poetry, a degree of freedom was taught: the emphasis was placed on the sense of sentence, even at the expense of lexical exactitude. In order to convey the Bridegroom's reluctance, Hugo compared him to someone fleeing from the tusks of a boar: "Quem fulmineo dente lacessit aper" (Whom a boar has wounded with a shiny tooth; I, 7, v. 16). Lacki's rendition uses the image of a bison sweating from the charge; after all, the point was to convey the image of fleeing in extreme terror rather than zoological details. In employing his predecessor's rhyme, Żaba came close to the original, and yet—although he mentions fleeing from a wild boar—he never mentions its tusks. Żaba strays from the original nearly as often in other instances, while remaining close to Lacki's rendition. Thus, the choice of translational solutions was determined not so much by philological fidelity as by the clarity of the Polish version.

All three translators took due care about mastery of expression. For instance, they were careful to render compound epithets such as "astriferos" (wearing stars, I, 12, v. 13), "trisulca" (tricorder, I, 12, v. 14), "aurifluis" (flowing of gold,

---

179   Copy of the National Library in Warsaw, call no. XVIII.1.5687.
180   Copy of the National Museum in Kraków, call no. VIII–XVIII.1751.

III, 6, v. 25), characteristic of the elevated style, in their Polish translations. Sometimes they proposed their own solutions, such as the replacement of "clam tacitis" (secretly quiet; introductory emblem, v. 1) with "tajnosmutne" (secretly sorrowful) (Lacki) or "tria deliciis" (triply delightful, III, 6, v. 7) with "potrójnie śliczne" (triply beautiful) (Żaba); in other cases, they turned to *compositae* that had no counterparts in the original but were popular in Polish poetry, such as "prędkolotny" (nimbleswift), coined by the anonymous translator of elegy III, 6 (v. 55).

Lacki occasionally made discreet references to the Polish lyrical tradition. His rendition of Hugo's couplet recalling a sky studded with stars like precious stones (III, 6, vv. 59–60): "O coelum, o coelum, o gemmantia lumina stellae, / o nisi sidereis, atria digna choris" (Oh heavens, oh heavens, oh shining lights of stars, oh tabernacles only of starry choirs worthy) reads: "O niebiosa gwiazdami ślicznie aftowane, / O gmachy czystym tylko duchom zgotowane" (Oh skies splendidly embroidered with stars, oh buildings furnished solely for pure spirits)—referring to *Hymn to God* by the foremost Polish Renaissance poet, Jan Kochanowski (1530–84), so well known to his readers: "Tyś Pan wszytkiego świata, Tyś niebo zbudował / I złotemi gwiazdami ślicznieś uhaftował" (Thou art Lord of all the world, thou didst build heaven and embroider it beautifully with golden stars).

The anonymous translator of elegy III, 6 recognized the allusion and went a step further in his version, replacing the rhyme with one that was even closer to Kochanowski's.

Hugo used diminutives, as for example when referring to the bed of the cross as a little bed ("lectullus," II, 10, vv. 19, 21, 22, 38, 53, 54) or dubbing the Soul an earthly proprietor that tenderly boasts of her little hamlet ("villula," II, 7, vv. 45–46). Polish translators followed his suggestion. In addition, Lacki introduced an accumulation of hypocorisms in the description of the Soul caressing a little boy whom she holds in her arms, an excerpt that one would seek in vain in the Latin original (II, 9, vv. 63–68, 79–80)[181] and, consequently, in Żaba's translation. Such accumulations of tenderness can be found in Stanisław Grochowski's (1542–1612) carol in order to touch the reader through hypocorisms conveying the infancy of Jesus.[182] Lacki used this procedure to achieve the same artistic purpose.

---

181   Mirosława Hanusiewicz, *Święte i zmysłowe w poezji religijnej polskiego baroku* (Lublin: Wydawnictwo KUL, 1998), 250–52; Dietz, Stronks, and Zawadzka, "Rooms-katholieke *Pia desideria*," 36–37.

182   Andrzej de Vincenz, "Kilka uwag o stylu poetyckim XVI wieku od Kochanowskiego do Grochowskiego," in *Fragen der polnischen Kultur im 16. Jahrhundert*, ed. Reinhold Olesch and Hans Rothe (Giessen: W. Schmitz, 1980), 269–74.

Conversely, one of the hallmarks of Żaba's translation are fictional utterances that take the form of *oratio recta* and feature much more frequently in the translation than in the original. Short statements in direct speech were intended to lend verve to the translation. To this end, the translator usually cropped a line or two from the original (e.g., I, 12, vv. 7–8; 14, vv. 67–68; II, 15, vv. 7–10; III, 6, vv. 17–18; 33–34). Hugo eagerly made erudite references not only to biblical characters but also to mythological or ancient ones. Seasoned by their school practice, Lacki and Żaba had no problems with this subject matter, freely modifying realities when necessary to make them resonate better in the Polish text. Thus, they would replace Gradivus with Mars, and Notos's raptures with Neptune's wrath. Perhaps the same was true of the anonymous translator. If so, the nun took the allusions poorly, as in her opinion they were unbecoming of the religious subject matter of his work. While her version retains the mention of the gold-bearing Indian river (III, 6, v. 30), the comparison to Hercules, who held up the sky instead of Atlas (vv. 43–44), or the erudite mention of Alexander the Great (356–323 BCE) (vv. 69–70), taken from Plutarch (*Alexander* 5.4), were omitted.

Whether through the fault of the anonymous translator or the nun editor who incorporated his work into her poem, the *Na słowa "Psalmu siedmdziesiątego wtórego" przydatek* occasionally demonstrates a different valorization of the theme than the one present in the Latin original. In the elegy, the Soul seeks treasures underground, in the sea, and in heaven, all of which ultimately turn out to be nothing without God. And while Hugo did not condemn the worldly charms that pleased the Soul (III, 6, vv. 11–14), in the nun's version any delight in the world is stigmatized with pejorative epithets, while the passage stating that one's need for God will not be quenched even by traversing the whole world is supplanted by a passage about the world being worthless (vv. 11–14): "Przyznawam, iżeście mię zdrożnie uwodziły, / Długoście sercem moim kłamliwie łudziły, / Ale chociażbym teraz i wszytek świat miała, / Wszytek bym jako błoto pod nogą deptała" (I admit that you have deceived me wickedly, deceived my heart for a long time, but even if I were to gain the whole world even now, I would trample it like mud).

The rhymes of Lacki and the monastic translator are more accurate, while approximation rhymes are more typical of Żaba's work. Access to the two redactions of his text proves that the poet was aware of the fact and strove to make corrections as part of his editorial work. Żaba also occasionally resorts to moving the word stress to the ultimate syllable before the caesura. These may be nuances, but they suggest that Lacki and the anonymous translator were more adept at the technical side of poetry writing than Żaba.

Minor deviations from the original can be found with all three translators. Therefore, it is worth emphasizing that, given the standards in this regard back in the seventeenth and eighteenth centuries, all three displayed a high level of translational expertise. Although only Lacki was praised for his translation by his contemporaries—the poet Kochowski celebrated him for his "extremely ornate poetic style," while the chronicler Komoniecki commended him for "translating in highly artful and elegant verse"—similar praise is also due to the other two translators.

5 Translations and Adaptations of Exegetical Excerpts from *Pia desideria*

5.1 The Demand for Translations of Treatises by the Doctors of the Church

The exegetical works of the fathers of the church, indispensable in the interpretation of the more challenging passages of the scriptures, and hence treasured by Catholic and Protestant theologians, were translated into Polish starting in the sixteenth century. Initially, they comprised single treatises, minor in terms of volume.[183] In the early seventeenth century, the first anthologies of patristic authors began to appear in print. The year 1609 saw the release of a translation of excerpts from the works of St. Bonaventure,[184] while 1630 brought a collection of excerpts from the writings of St. Bernard of Clairvaux.[185] In turn, 1617 witnessed the publication of the first Polish translation of five treatises attributed to St. Augustine: *Liber meditationum, Liber soliloquiorum animae ad Deum, Manuale* (Manual), *De contritione cordis* (On contrition of the heart) and *De vanitate saeculi* (On the vanity of the century). The author of the translation, which became very popular, was the Jesuit professor of rhetoric in Nesvizh, Jan Aland (1559–1641).[186]

While the translation of excerpts from St. Bernard of Clairvaux was addressed to consecrated readers, the translation of Pseudo-Augustine's writings targeted a broader audience and thus lived to see two reprints in the first

---

183   See Janina Czerniatowicz and Czesław Mazur, *Recepcja antyku chrześcijańskiego w Polsce: Materiały bibliograficzne*, vol. 1, *XV–XVIII w.*, part 1, *Autorzy i teksty* (Lublin: TNKUL, 1978).

184   *Pochodnia duchowna [...] wyjęta z ksiąg ś[więtego] Bonawentury* (Kraków: Mikołaj Lob, 1609).

185   Michał Brokard Melecius, trans., *Sposób mądrego i dobrego życia na świecie [...] od ś[więtego] Bernata* (Kraków: Franciszek Cezary, 1630).

186   Aureliusz Augustyn, *Ksiąg pięcioro*, trans. [Jan Aland] (Vilnius: Akademia Jezuicka, 1617).

half of the seventeenth century alone, while also being reprinted on multiple occasions subsequently. That it was read with great fervor by consecrated readers is demonstrated by *Piosneczka serca skruszonego z słów ś[więtego] Augustyna* (The song of a contrite heart from the words of St. Augustine), known from Carmelite manuscripts. The anonymous author has rehearsed in this hymn the paragraphs of Pseudo-Augustine's *Liber meditationum* (39:5–7), faithfully following Aland's translation.[187] The same passage that caught the attention of the author of the *Piosneczka serca skruszonego* was included in *Pia desideria*, in a set of excerpts commenting on emblem 1, 10, and its spellings were included in Polish Carmelite adaptations, both in *Wzdychania pobożne* (I, 10.10) and *Pragnienia Dusze pobożnej* (I, 10.10). In both cases—duly discussed in the subsequent sections of this Part—the authors of the Polish versions also consulted Aland's translation, commonly used in monastic circles.

5.2   Carmelite Provenance of Polish Adaptations

Translations of the works of the doctors of the church and their reprints are a testament to the popularity enjoyed by patristic literature. As a matter of fact, the popularity of *Pia desideria* among consecrated readers was significantly influenced by the author's fortunate decision to supplement poetic subscriptions with excerpts from the exegetical commentaries by the doctors of the church. The poetic artistry and erudition of Hugo's elegies mainly captivated lay readers, and consequently, the Polish translations were the work of Lithuanian magnates, Lacki and Żaba; those living in enclosed cloisters were mostly attracted to the excerpts from exegetical works. However, this group was primarily composed of male recipients who knew Latin. Command of the language among nuns was limited to choristers, whom monks taught rudimentary Latin, but even those sisters would at times confuse words when reading Latin.[188] Thus, there was a pressing need to translate the essential parts of Hugo's tome, which—in the case of nuns—consisted of biblical verses and exegetical commentaries penned by established church authorities.

The need to have Hugo's work translated into a national language was not limited to Poland. In 1629, with Hugo's permission, the first Dutch translation of *Pia desideria* by de Harduwijn, titled *Goddelycke wenschen* (J.680/N.357), was published by Aertssens's printing house. The translation included Latin inscriptions, the entirety of the commentaries drawn from the writings of the fathers of the church, as well as paraphrased poetic subscriptions. Aertssens

---

187   Grześkowiak, Gwioździk, and Nowicka-Struska, *Karmelitańskie adaptacje* Pia desideria, 29–30.

188   Gil, *Żywot Zadzikowej*, 153.

took care to embellish the volume with prints of Bolswert's original copper-plates, which were in his possession. In the successive reprints of the translation, dated 1632 (J.681) and 1645 (J.682/N.358), the lyrical subscriptions were overlooked. They were limited to exegetical excerpts decorated with woodcut copies of the original engravings, made by van Sichem the Younger. These changes suggest that admirers of religious-themed elegies were not the largest group to whom the vernacular versions of *Pia desideria* were addressed.

The individuals who were most interested in the edition limited to illustrated commentaries on selected verses can be identified thanks to the aforementioned Dutch manuscript, transcribed by a nun before 1666.[189] It featured excerpts from a said translation of *Pia desideria*, illustrated with copies of Bolswert's original copperplate engravings. The copyist not only chose quotations that were pertinent to her needs; in the case of the paragraphs of Pseudo-Augustine's *Liber soliloquiorum animae ad Deum*, she also used a different vernacular version of them, the popular Dutch translation by Antonius van Hemert (d. *c*.1560).[190] Analogous phenomena can be identified in the Polish reception of this part of Hugo's volume: Polish translators of exegetical passages in the case of Pseudo-Augustine's writings (not only his *Soliloquies*) have used the acclaimed Aland's translation and, whenever possible, strove to complement their manuscripts with engravings adopted from *Pia desideria*.

A total of three different Polish versions of the exegetical excerpts of the *Pia desideria* are known, all compiled specifically for Discalced Carmelite nuns. This female congregation, which first appeared in the Polish–Lithuanian state in 1612, was characterized by a high intellectual standard and a focus on ecstatic experiences. The first generations of Polish Discalced Carmelite nuns were among the vanguard of ardent early modern piety and placed great emphasis on the spiritual development of nuns. When, in the second half of the seventeenth century, they began to compose devotional songs in large numbers, one of the most common themes involved affectionate monologues of the Soul addressed to the mystical Bridegroom. It is hardly surprising, therefore, that adaptations of Hugo's volume found devoted readers among the sisters of this congregation.

Since the Discalced Carmelite nunneries were under the jurisdiction of male convents, the monks maintained continuous contact with the nuns, acting as their confessors and spiritual guides. The intellectual and literary aspirations of the Discalced Carmelite monks meant that they were well equipped

---

189 Manuscript kept at the Universiteitsbibliotheek, Radboud Universiteit in Nijmegen, call no. 325.

190 Dietz, "Media Literate Catholics," 12–14.

to perform the demanding tasks of translation, while the spiritual care they exercised fostered the creation of formative works, which laid out the principles behind the pursuit of spiritual perfection for the nuns. Such was also the purpose of the three Polish translations of *Pia desideria*: *Wzdychania pobożne*, *Strzały serdeczne*, and *Pragnienia Dusze pobożnej*.

5.3 Translations of Excerpts

There are two known Polish translations of the excerpts collected in *Pia desideria*. One was based on the full set of excerpts compiled by Hugo, while the basis for the second was an abridgment compiled for van Haestens's 1628 reissue (reprinted many times in the subsequent years), which reduced the extensive sets of quotations accompanying each emblem to a single one, spanning a maximum of two sentences.

5.3.1 The Translation of the Full Version: *Wzdychania pobożne* (Pious Sighs)

The complete anthology of excerpts from the exegetical commentaries included in Hugo's collection proved to be of interest to just one translator. His work proves that he had prior experience in interpreting theological texts. The text of the translation has survived in the form of an extensive notebook.[191] The nature of the handwriting indicates that the codex was written in the second half of the seventeenth or in the early eighteenth century. A sizable portion of the scribe's errors are evident errors of the eye. They prove that the manuscript is not an autograph but merely a copy of a prior translation. Following the translation is the copyist's formula, "For the glory of God and for the encouragement of pious hearts to love the heavenly Bridegroom," indicating his mobilizing intention. The codex only contains the text of the translation, lacks the title page, and, consequently, the original title. Based on the headings of the respective books, one can surmise that the title may have read *Wzdychania pobożne*.

The Polish text consists of a translation of the biblical inscriptions accompanying the individual emblems, along with the exegetical commentaries compiled by Hugo.[192] This is not a complete translation of all the excerpts but a comprehensive selection of them. Of the 619 original paragraphs, the translator eliminated 126. In general, the omissions included short quotations, hence the significant number of abridgments did not cause major damage to the text. In each successive book, the number of omitted quotations steadily decreases:

---

191 Manuscript kept at the library of the Discalced Carmelite convent in Kraków (Wesoła), call no. 204.

192 Quotations from *Wzdychania pobożne* after: Grześkowiak, Gwioździk and Nowicka-Struska, *Karmelitańskie adaptacje* Pia desideria, 77–275.

in book 1, it amounts to fifty-three (22.4 percent) of the 236 original paragraphs; in book 2, forty-one (twenty-one percent) out of a total of 195 quotations were left out; in book 3, the omission ratio drops down to thirty-two (16.7 percent) out of 188. This tendency indicates that the omissions cannot be attributed to the translator's fatigue; rather, they were the result of a deliberate translation strategy, in particular given that the reduction in excerpts was not limited to the selection of individual passages.

The inclusion of a given excerpt in the translation does not mean that the translator rendered it in full. In fact, the translator did not shy away from abridgments. In most cases, these included up to several words, although on some occasions the excerpts included in the original version of *Pia desideria* were stripped down to single sentences (usually initial or final), provided that it explicitly captured the issue discussed in the entire paragraph. The translator also consistently overlooked poetic quotations from the didactic verses of St. Gregory of Nazianzus (*c.*329–90) or St. Paulinus of Nola (*c.*354–431), apparently lacking the vocation to translate poetry. In the end, the translation covers roughly eighty percent of the excerpts, and the omissions usually concern the passages whose content was redundant with respect to the translated quotations. Thanks to these abridgments, the Polish translation benefited from the condensation of exegetical musings.

The translation demonstrates not only the linguistic competence of the translator, most likely a Discalced Carmelite friar but also his considerable ability to render theological texts. The author did not lose track of the occasionally intricate syntax of the original, avoided additions, and did not obscure the nuances of the argument but instead conveyed them neatly in Polish.

Another testament to the quality of the friar's craft is the fact that he employed Aland's translations of Pseudo-Augustine's writings. The anonymous translator exploited them in a manner likely acquired in school rhetoric classes, where as part of synonymy exercises students learned, among other things, how to paraphrase assigned texts by means of redaction. Collating his predecessor's translation with the original text (one should note that the translator appositely identified the relevant passages in Aland's print even in those instances where Hugo located them incorrectly), he tried to replace as many words as possible with their synonyms. However, these lexical substitutions never once violated the structure of the sentences, which consistently benefited from Aland's syntactic solutions in the new version. As a result, the translator's work reveals both a clear influence of the 1617 translation and an emulative effort to ensure that the final outcome of the redactions resulted in qualitative changes.

Hugo supplied the poems in the *Pia desideria* collection with numbers but without accompanying them with any generic designations. His decision induced Polish translators and adaptors to devise their own terminology in this regard. The translator of *Wzdychania pobożne* referred to them as "pictures," as had Mieleszko, who referred to his own compositions based on engravings as "paintings." However, unlike in Mieleszko's adaptations, in *Wzdychania pobożne* one would struggle to find any connections to the *Pia desideria* images beyond these pseudo-generic designations. The translator was not interested in the engravings or the elegiac subscriptions of the Jesuit scholar, instead focusing exclusively on the inspired words of the biblical books and the holy doctors of the church.

5.3.2   Translation of the Abridged Version: *Strzały serdeczne* (Heartfelt Arrows)

Monastic audiences also appreciated the abridged version of the exegetical excerpts. Its translation was preserved in one of the Carmelite *silva rerum*. It was a manuscript of modest proportions, originally containing more than 403 pages, of which only 127 have survived.[193] Unfortunately, the codex was lost several years ago (a digital copy was used as a basis for the modern edition).

In addition to the Polish translation of *Canticum Canticorum* (Song of Songs) and excerpts from St. John Climacus's (*c.*579–649) treatise *Scala paradisi* (Ladder of paradise; sixth–seventh century), the manuscript contained a collection of texts by Carmelite authors, including translations of the writings of St. Teresa of Ávila (1515–82), St. John of the Cross (1542–91), St. John of Ávila (1500–69), and St. Mary Magdalene de' Pazzi (1566–1607). The manuscript also contained a number of signed works by Polish Carmelite authors, most by Fr. Stefan of St. Teresa (Hieronim Kucharski [1595–1653]) and Mother Anna of Jesus (Jadwiga Stobieńska [1593–1649]).

The manuscript was transcribed by a Discalced Carmelite nun, Mother Agnieszka Konstancja of Lord Jesus the Lamb (Konstancja Iżycka [1636–1723]), known as an excellent calligrapher. As per the nun's biography, written shortly after her death: "The reverend mother was blessed with fine handwriting, which everyone took care of as if it were a relic, and whoever acquired it, treasures it greatly as a token of remembrance of the mother and her piety."[194] The sheets of paper pasted into Carmelite hymnal, containing the lyrics of individual hymns and copied with utmost care, prove that this statement was not an exaggeration. Sister Agnieszka's calligraphic talent resulted in her

---

193   Before it got lost, the manuscript had been kept at the Archives of the Province of the Discalced Carmelites in Kraków, call no. 246.

194   Onufry od Wniebowzięcia NMP (Tomasz Ośmielski), *Konterfekt życia przykładnego* (Kraków: Michał Dyaszewski, 1747), 330.

being eagerly entrusted with transcribing the formative works contained in the codex in question.

The discussed manuscript may have been drawn up in the early 1650s at the earliest (Iżycka took her vows in the last days of 1653), while the *terminus ante quem* can be dated to 1669, which saw the canonization of Mary Magdalene de' Pazzi (in the manuscript, she was still referred to as "blessed"). The approximate dating of the copy, which was drafted in the seventh decade of the seventeenth century at the latest, leads one to assume that the *Strzały serdeczne* translation had been written earlier. Indeed, its text is distorted by a number of major errors, proving that the surviving copy and the autograph translation must have been separated by at least several intermediate copies.

Strzały serdeczne is a translation of the biblical inscriptions of the *Pia desideria* and excerpts from the exegetical works of the doctors of the church, based on the radically abridged 1628 reissue. The anonymous translator has labeled his work with an original title—*Strzały serdeczne z "Pisma Świętego" i ojców świętych zrobione, a od Dusze nabożnej ku niebu wypuszczone* (Heartfelt arrows, made from the Scriptures and the writings of the holy fathers, and launched toward heaven by a pious Soul)—inspired by the engraving accompanying the collection's introductory emblem, depicting arrows equipped with phylacteries inscribed with emotional exclamations coming out of the Soul's breast toward the divine addressee.[195]

Despite the compact size of the text (which takes up only twelve pages of the code), the piece speaks volumes about the translator's workshop. The professional approach can be seen in the use of the existing translations, which enjoyed a well-deserved reputation at the time. Polish translations of the biblical inscriptions in *Strzały serdeczne* were drawn from Wujek's 1599 rendition of the Scriptures. Similarly, the Carmelite translator relied on Aland's model translation when citing subscriptions from the works of Pseudo-Augustine. Unlike the author of the *Wzdychania pobożne*, in this case the interpreter made his best efforts to faithfully retain Aland's wording, limiting any changes to contemporizing the archaic lexis.

One characteristic feature of the style employed by the author of *Strzały serdeczne* is his tendency to amplify the translation with synonymous repetitions. He repeatedly duplicated single terms of the original, such as "amatores suos **conterit**"—"he **smashes** or **crushes** his admirers" (1, 4), "dissipatione **valida**"—"with a **strong** and **hard** toss" (1, 5), "culpam **fatetur**"—"she **confesses, reveals** guilt" (1, 12), and so on. These repetitions, of which the concise

---

195   Based on Grześkowiak, Gwioździk, and Nowicka-Struska, *Karmelitańskie adaptacje* Pia desideria, 277–93.

translation contains over thirty, are always tautological in nature, and their primary function was to increase the emphatic quality of a given statement.

Also striking is the translator's attention to the needs of the Carmelite nuns, to whom he addressed his translation. He specified all mentions of love in the text in such a way as to leave no doubt that it had nothing to do with carnal passion but concerned a spiritual affection for God. In keeping with this principle, the title of the third book, which originally reads "Suspiria Animae **amantis**" (Sighs of the loving soul), was translated into "Sighs of the Soul in **Love with God**"; similarly, in a paragraph borrowed from a commentary on the Song of Songs by Gilbert of Hoyland (1110–70), "Tenax est funiculus **amor**. **Amor** affectuose trahit [...]. Nihil **amoris** tenacius vinculo" (Love is a strong is cord. Love attracts affectionately. Nothing is stronger than the bond of love), the translator supplemented each instance of the word "amor" with an appropriate apposition: "Strong and powerful is the cord of the **Divine Love**. The **Divine Love** attracts all affections. Nothing is stronger than the bonds of the **Divine Love**" (II, 8).

Similarly, Polish appositions of the biblical verses concerning the Bride—feeble from love—with whom Carmelite nuns identified themselves, had an analogous genesis. In *Strzały serdeczne*, such references—despite the Vulgate and Hugo's citations, where the phrase "amore langveo" (I languish with love) is used—are complemented by a personal pronoun, specifying that it is not her affection to, but the affection bestowed on her by, the Divine Bridegroom that the author had in mind: "I adjure you, o daughters of Jerusalem, if you find my beloved, that you tell him that I languish with **his** love" (III, 1, inscription = Song 5:8) or "Stay me up with flowers, compass me about with apples, because I languish with **his** love" (III, 2, inscription = Song 2:5).

Strzały serdeczne represents the work of an author with strong translation skills and some artistic ambitions, who also strove to cater to the needs of the prospective target audience of his translation.

5.4   *Teofila Zadzikowa's Adaptation:* Pragnienia Dusze pobożnej (*Desires of a Pious Soul*)

Aside from the two translations, Carmelite manuscripts also contain a loose adaptation of Hugo's excerpts, which used them as a foundation for an autonomous work. The adaptation is known from two copies, one written down in the summer of 1662 and the other penned in the spring of 1697. Since the text of *Pragnienia Dusze pobożnej* is linked to the scenes depicted in the *Pia desideria* engravings, both handwritten copies were illustrated with cut-out engravings, although only in the second copy were the prints glued on solidly enough to survive to this day.

The earlier manuscript was written in Lublin. The title page of this compact volume bears the following title, expanded to include valuable information: *Książeczka "Pragnienia Dusze pobożnej" napisana w Lublinie, w klasztorze Niepokalanego Poczęcia Naś[większej] Panny, 1. dnia augusta r[oku] P[ańskiego] 1662* (Booklet "Desires of a pious Soul," transcribed in Lublin, at the monastery of the Immaculate Conception of the Blessed Virgin Mary, on August 1 of the year of our Lord 1662).[196] The distinctive handwriting proves that the text was copied by the twenty-six-year-old Carmelite nun of Lublin, Agnieszka of the Lord Jesus the Lamb, the very sister who transcribed the codex containing the text of *Strzały serdeczne*. On this occasion, too, she took great care to ensure a high aesthetic standard: the text bears highlights in red ink (including chapter numbers, initials of the respective inscriptions and chapters, and the biblical references of the inscriptions) and was inscribed in the boxes delineated by linear frames. The codex was originally provided with engravings, which were subsequently peeled off, with none surviving to this day. In the manuscript, the boxes for insets with engravings were surrounded by linear frames. Since their dimensions (41/69 × 38/45 mm) are smaller than those of the engravings adorning the editions printed before 1662, the engravings had to be appropriately cropped, which resulted in them also being stripped of their Latin inscriptions (the same was true of the illustrations in the second manuscript of *Pragnienia Dusze pobożnej*).

The women readers of the manuscript annotated it in a fashion that enables one to outline its history. The earliest note indicates the adaptation's possible author, and as such I will discuss it last. Another note proves that, following its use by the Carmelite nuns of Lublin, the codex became the property of a layperson. One of the first pages bears the signature of Elżbieta Febronia Koniecpolska née Rzewuska (d. after 1721), renowned for her piety. How the magnate came into possession of the manuscript is easy to infer. The five sisters of Elżbieta's husband, Grand Equerry of the Crown and Sieradz Voivod Jan Aleksander Koniecpolski (1635–1719), took the monastic habit. As part of his will, Koniecpolski bequeathed eighteen thousand florins to one of these women, a Discalced Carmelite nun living at the Lublin convent. Given the importance of the transcribed work and the aesthetic quality of the codex, the

---

196   Manuscript kept at the Vasyl Stefanyk National Scientific Library of Ukraine in Lviv, Rare Book Division, call no. CT I 118348. For a detailed codicological and calligraphic analysis of this codex, see the article by Ewa Zielińska, "Rękopis Lwowskiej Narodowej Naukowej Biblioteki Ukrainy im. Wasyla Stefanyka, sygn. CT I 118348: Pamiątka po karmelitankach bosych z klasztoru Niepokalanego Poczęcia NMP w Lublinie," *Studia archiwalne* 7 (2020): 91–129.

manuscript booklet may have been the perfect token of the nun's gratitude for such a generous donation.

In the subsequent years, the manuscript wound up at the library of the Benedictine nunnery at All Saints' Church in Lviv, with whom Elżbieta Koniecpolska maintained cordial relations. Among the Benedictine nuns at the Lviv convent were her sister, Marianna Zofia Rzewuska (d.1709), as well as her niece Anna Rzewuska (c.1695–1730) and cousin Anna Rzewuska (d.1702). It was thanks to them that the Lviv cloister came into possession of a range of volumes owned by Koniecpolska; consequently, one can assume that the Lublin manuscript was Koniecpolska's gift to one of her relatives.

In the wake of the convent's liquidation in 1946, part of its book collection, including the manuscript of *Pragnienia Dusze pobożnej*, was transferred to the library currently named the Vasyl Stefanyk Lviv National Scientific Library of Ukraine.

The earliest provenance note at the end of the codex is the work of Mother Teresa Barbara of the Blessed Sacrament (Teofila Zadzikowa née Kretkowska [1609–70]) herself; it was made in the same ink as the codex, so probably still in 1662. The note states: "For the work, I ask you to save my soul after my passing by ordering a Mass and saying prayers in my intention. Teresa Barbara of the Blessed Sacrament." The mother did not specify what kind of work she had in mind. It certainly did not involve rewriting the codex, since that was the work of another sister. She also likely did not mean her work for the Discalced Carmelite nuns of Lublin, who owed a great deal to the then fifty-four-year-old mother, who had served as prioress for three terms. This appears to be how the author of the copied work presented herself.

Teofila Zadzikowa, the eldest daughter of the Brześć Kujawski Voivod Andrzej Kretkowski (d.1643) and Jadwiga née Tylicka (b. c.1580), desired to become a nun from an early age. However, her parents married her off, against her will, to the standard bearer of Sieradz, Jan Zadzik (d.1632). It was only after her husband's death that Jadwiga fulfilled her intention and entered St. Joseph's Convent in Lublin. In 1649, she was appointed superior of the newly built Monastery of the Immaculate Conception of the Blessed Virgin Mary, located two blocks away. In 1665, she was one of the four founding sisters who went to establish a new congregation of Discalced Carmelites in Poznań. Outspoken, ambitious, and a good organizer, she was one of the most outstanding personalities among the first Polish Discalced Carmelite nuns.[197]

---

197   Czesław Gil, *Słownik polskich karmelitanek bosych 1612–1914* (Kraków: Wydawnictwo Karmelitów Bosych, 1999), 61–64; Gil, "Nauki o życiu zakonnym m. Anny Stobieńskiej oraz m. Teresy Barbary Zadzikowej, karmelitanek bosych," *Nasza przeszłość* 105 (2006): 43–116, here 46–48.

A substantial number of texts penned by Zadzikowa have survived, including spiritual reports, acts of prayer, and short teachings, written with flair and in plain style, revealing her theological erudition.[198] The monastic author of her biography attested to Zadzikowa's literary passion in the following words:

> The Lord bestowed upon her a great gift of wisdom and understanding of divine matters, so that she could write books. And when she showed certain prayers—which she complied into a booklet for her personal use to aid her in performing devotions—to one of our reverend fathers [a Discalced Carmelite], an excellent theologian, he said: "There is not a single error here, on the contrary, it conforms to the mystical theology taught by the holy church."[199]

All of the above indicates that the author of *Pragnienia Dusze pobożnej* was Mother Teresa Barbara of the Blessed Sacrament.

It is possible that she not only compiled the work and initiated the production of its clean copy in 1662 but also had a hand in its destruction. The glue-stained slots that once bore the engravings prove that the codex originally contained forty-seven engravings cut out from the *Pia desideria* volume. Their removal can be considered evidence of the particular attractiveness of the engravings and a kind of testimony to the reception of the illustrated manuscript. In this context, it worth noting the episode reported in Zadzikowa's biography, which took place during her meeting with Queen Marie Louise Gonzaga (1611–67) in 1665: "As she bid farewell to the queen, Mother Barbara presented her with two pictures from her little booklet she had with her. The queen was very grateful for them and ordered her to sign both, which she did."[200]

Whether Zadzikowa's "little booklet" was the same as "Booklet *Desires of a pious Soul*" is unclear, and yet the quoted passage constitutes another instance of a peculiar recycling practice, which involved peeling off engravings so that they could independently inspire religious musings in subsequent recipients.

The second copy of the work bears different information on the title page, *Książeczka "Pragnienia Dusze pobożnej" napisana dnia 12 kwietnia r[oku] 1697 dla wielebnych panien karmelitanek konwentu warszawskiego* (Booklet "Desires of a pious Soul," transcribed on April 12, 1697 for the reverend Carmelite nuns of the Warsaw convent; fig. 12).[201] The title indicates that the codex was copied

---

198   Gil, "Nauki o życiu zakonnym," 72–116.
199   *Żywot Zadzikowej*, 157–58.
200   *Żywot Zadzikowej*, 217.
201   Manuscript kept at the library of the Discalced Carmelite convent in Kraków (Wesoła), call no. 121.

FIGURE 12   Title page of a manuscript copy of *Pragnienia Dusze pobożnej* from 1697
(manuscript of the Library of the Discalced Carmelite convent in Kraków
[Wesoła])

at another convent, with the nuns of the Warsaw convent in mind, while the subsequent provenance note added to the manuscript confirms that it made its way to the intended addressees. An analysis of the text proves that the 1697 manuscript is a copy (indirect or direct) of the 1662 Lublin manuscript.

The meticulously transcribed text was decorated with forty-seven engravings cut out from a copy of *Pia desideria*; all of them have survived. A frontispiece pasted on the title page certifies that the copperplate engravings were cut from an edition combining two different works by Jesuit authors, Hugo's *Pia desideria* and Matthäus Rader (1561–1634) and Johann Niess's (1584–1634) 1626 poem *Quatuor hominis ultima* (Man's four last things). The two works were first published in a single volume by the Cologne typographer Konstantin Münich (d.1664), who printed it in 1635 (J.638). The combined book was subsequently reprinted by 1673 by Johann Karl Münich (b.1639; J.653), in the same printing house. Another reprint, released in 1682 and typeset at the Cologne printing house run by the widow and heirs of Johann Anton Kinckius (1649–79; J.657), used a frontispiece that was slightly different from the previous one, and it was this second frontispiece that was used to decorate the title page of the codex copied for the Warsaw Carmelite nuns.

The new variant of the frontispiece was used in three reprints of the Cologne printing press, dated 1682 (J.657), 1694 (J.659/G.365), and 1709 (J.666/G.366), respectively. Since the Warsaw manuscript of *Pragnienia Dusze pobożnej* was decorated with engravings in 1697, they may have come only from the first or second of the aforementioned editions. A comparison of the makeup of inscriptions under the opening engravings (for the Cologne editions, the copperplate illustrations were made without inscriptions, which were typeset separately for each successive reissue) proves that they were clipped from the edition printed in Cologne in 1682 (J.657). In the Cologne editions, the engravings were not copied from Bolswert's original copperplates but from the modified imitations that first adorned the 1628 edition of *Pia desideria* published by van Haestens.

Based on biblical inscriptions and exegetical excerpts, the text of *Pragnienia Dusze pobożnej* was also inspired by *Pia desideria* engravings. Zadzikowa expanded this inventive material to include works relevant to Carmelite spirituality, using them as a reference for an original work of a formative nature.[202]

The Carmelite nun of Lublin did not translate the biblical verses indicated by Hugo on her own but instead consulted Wujek's rendition of the Vulgate. In the seventeenth century, this official Catholic translation of the scriptures was

---

202   Based on Grześkowiak, Gwioździk, and Nowicka-Struska, *Karmelitańskie adaptacje* Pia desideria, 295–489.

regarded as the stylistic golden standard of biblical Polish. On the other hand, the author of *Pragnienia Dusze pobożnej* used original quotations from exegetical works in a different way than the translations discussed above. Out of the dozen-or-so or twenty-odd passages used as commentary to each emblem, she usually cited only a few. The author's preference was clear in this regard. She most fondly invoked the authority of Augustine of Hippo (eighteen instances) and Bernard of Clairvaux (fourteen), followed by the likes of Bonaventure of Bagnoregio (seven), Gregory the Great (seven), Ambrose of Milan (seven), Jerome of Stridon (two), Thomas Aquinas (1224/25–74) (one), and Prospero of Aquitaine (c.390–c.455) (one); among the Greek authors, the translator's favorites included John Chrysostom (three), Gregory of Nazianzus (two), and Basil the Great (330–79) (one). Thus, the top of the list was occupied by the doctors of the church, whose collected writings were among the first to be translated into Polish: Pseudo-Augustine, St. Bernard, and St. Bonaventure. Carmelite writers frequently relied on the authority of the other authors in the above list, too.

Although the author of *Pragnienia Dusze pobożnej* eagerly invoked church authorities—"Let us cry out with St. Augustine" (II, 1.9), "According to St. Bernard" (II, 2.5), "As per St. Gregory" (II, 1.6)—she was in fact reluctant to let their work speak for itself. The citations thus announced only occasionally constitute translations of Latin passages. One exception to this rule concerns quotations from the works of Pseudo-Augustine. Even in the case of heavily amplified paraphrases, it is evident that the Carmelite author relied on Aland's translation. The other holy authors were less fortunate. In general, Zadzikowa formulated the thoughts attributed to them independently, regarding the Latin texts as thematic prompts. The same is true of the remaining paragraphs of her adaptations. Although they lack indications that they were inspired by Hugo's excerpts, most are derived from the Jesuit's text; however, the affinity is often reduced to a mere thematic commonality. Zadzikowa used other authors' thoughts, considerably re-dressed and significantly processed in relation to the original, to create her own line of argument. Such carelessness in the approach to the Latin original indicates that the author's command of Latin was limited.

The liberal and selective use of exegetical excerpts is not the lone characteristic feature of Zadzikowa's adaptation, whose structure resembles that of a cento. Zadzikowa readily incorporated formative Carmelite texts into the text of the work. Chapter I, 6 begins with a lecture by Origen (c.185–c.253), taken from Hugo's volume, on the fighting gear of Satan, juxtaposed with the elements of the armor donned by the soldier of Christ, known from the Letter to the Ephesians. To highlight the oppositions indicated, the author of *Pragnienia Dusze pobożnej* listed the elements of the godly armament (I, 6.13). The direct inspiration for this paragraph, however, was neither Origen's treatise nor the epistle attributed to St. Paul but rather the 1635 Polish version of the earliest Carmelite constitution.[203] Zadzikowa used the translation of the same excerpt in her *Wykład na ponkt reguły naszej "O napominaniu"* (Explanation on the item of our rule "Concerning admonishment"),[204] and her biographer confirmed that this very item of the Rule was particularly dear to Mother Superior's heart: "She used to say, 'Even if the Soul would read no other books than our holy Rule, as long as this one point alone was observed, it would quickly and significantly approach holiness, for therein lies the salutary teaching that pertains to everything.'"[205]

Particularly prominent among the authorities cited by Zadzikowa are two Carmelite reformers, St. Teresa of Ávila and St. John of the Cross. Copies of their writings, purchased in print and reproduced as handwritten copies, were at the top of the reading list of any Discalced Carmelite nun. Therefore, some of the best-known statements by these two authors are referenced repeatedly in the chapters of the last book, dedicated to the confessions of the Soul at the most advanced stage on the path to union with God (III, 2.2; 3.2; 12.4).

The translator eagerly incorporated poetic paragraphs into her text. The references to the heavenly Jerusalem present in Hugo's emblem II, 15 prompted her to quote a lengthy, nearly one hundred-line praise of the Empyrean heaven, a translation of St. Pietro Damiani's (1007–72) *Hymnus de gloria paradisi caelestis* (Hymn on the glory of heavenly paradise), which was, let us add right away, a translation by a different author at that. Since Damiani's hymn was included in the twenty-sixth book of Pseudo-Augustine's treatise *Liber meditationum*, it was translated into Polish along with the entire work by Aland, and it was precisely this rendition that Zadzikowa transcribed in *Pragnienia Dusze pobożnej*.

A separate portion of the adaptation was reserved for poetic fragments from the literary output of St. Teresa of Ávila, cited on several occasions as the highest authority. These quotations were primarily derived from the Polish translations of her famous *Vivo sin vivir en mí* (I live without living in me). Polish Carmelite nuns readily paraphrased the song of their spiritual mother. The author of *Pragnienia Dusze pobożnej* used two out of several Polish translations.[206] Several other poetic quotations come from *Kantyka* (the Canticle), a song by

---

203 *Reguła i konstytucyje zakonnic karmelitanek bosych* (Kraków: wdowa i dziedzice Andrzeja Piotrkowczyka, 1635), 8–9.

204 Gil, "Nauki o życiu zakonnym," 72–73.

205 *Żywot Zadzikowej*, 157.

206 Mirosława Hanusiewicz, "Polskie barokowe przekłady i adaptacje *Glosy* św. Teresy z Avila," in *Barok polski wobec Europy: Sztuka przekładu*, ed. Alina Nowicka-Jeżowa and Marek Prejs (Warsaw: Anta, 2005), 241–57.

an anonymous Carmelite nun, likewise inspired by the theme of the desire for death studied in *Vivo sin vivir en mí*. It is apparent that the rhymed passages found their way into the adaptation not for their poetic charm but on account of their holy authors, Damiani and Teresa of Ávila, and the importance of their message: in the case of the hymn, it was admiration for the wonder of the heavenly Jerusalem; in the case of St. Teresa's *Vivo sin vivir en mí*, a Carmelite version of the Art of Dying Well.

While writing her work, Zadzikowa also readily drew inspiration from the *Pia desideria* engravings. Explicit references to the depicted scenes can be found in chapters o, I, 6, 9, 11–14, II, 1, 2, 4, 10, 13, 14, III, 1, 4, 5, 9–11. The author of *Pragnienia Dusze pobożnej* did not limit herself to references to the props depicted in the emblematic images. Whenever possible, she aimed to interpret them symbolically. For example, in the image of emblem III, 4, which Bolswert designed to accompany the inscription, "I to my beloved, and his turning is toward me" (Song 7:10), the Soul is presented holding a compass in her hands, whose needle points to the radiant face of the Divine Love. And while the exegetical quotations compiled by Hugo never once mention the compass, the evocative copperplate, which inspired the poetic commentaries of Mieleszko and Morsztyn, did leave its mark on the Carmelite author's imagery, too (III, 4.5 and 7):

> A ray shining from the Lord's face struck the center of my Soul, infected me with love, allowed me to learn the truth. It became my magnet, attracting me like a blade of grass [...]. Do not turn back, but ever look your Savior directly in the face, and the ray from his face will enlighten, adorn, and fill the compass of your conscience with purity.

In this instance, the Divine Love is not only a magnet attracting the Soul (the author mistakenly equated magnetic attraction with electrostatic attraction, for in fact a magnet would not attract a blade of grass, and yet the writer's intention was clear); the compass was also identified as a figure of conscience, which points one's moral choices in the right direction.

In her teachings to the novices, Zadzikowa emphasized that an image in and of itself is not worth much, unless provided with an interpretation: an engraving depicting Christ carrying the cross merely shows a bloodied man dragging a piece of wood. Only an explication of the pictorial meanings turns the scene into an interpretation of the mystery of salvation.[207] And since Zadzikowa was a seasoned interpreter of the significance behind emblematic engravings

---

207   Gil, "Nauki o życiu zakonnym," 104.

(suffice it to recall her interpretation of the illustrations in van Haeften's volume *Regia via crucis*), in *Pragnienia Dusze pobożnej* she took a great deal of liberty to offer her own interpretation of symbolic scenes, managing to assign meanings to the pictorial details that heightened the complex significance of a given representation.

References to the *Pia desideria* images are so vague that it is not easy to resolve which set of emblematic engravings was used by the author, that is, whether she consulted the original copperplate engravings by Bolswert (or a faithful copy thereof) or a second set of anonymous engravings known from van Haestens's edition (or a copy thereof), which differed from the original set in terms of iconographic solutions. Only one reference suggests that Zadzikowa drew from a volume illustrated with the original set of engravings. Bolswert's engraving for Emblem II, 2 shows the Soul in the midst of the dangerous labyrinth of the world, where deviating from the path leads one to a fatal fall into an abyss. In contrast, the corresponding illustration from the second set shows the Soul wandering around a small globe. As per the text of *Pragnienia Dusze pobożnej*, if one fails to strictly follow the guidance of the keeper of the Divine beacon, who points them in the right direction, one may fall into an abyss (II, 2.2). This passage thus refers to Bolswert's copperplate engravings, a fact worth noting since the engravings of the Cologne edition—preserved in a subsequent copy of the manuscript, drafted for the nuns of the Warsaw convent—invoke a different version of the copperplates.

The references to emblematic pictures, as well as the embellishment of the copied text with illustrations cut out from the printed volume, resulted from the desire to align the Polish version with meditative purposes to the fullest extent possible. Thus, the Discalced Carmelite nuns not only implemented the recommendations of the Ignatian model of spiritual exercises but also materialized the desiderata of their founder, St. Teresa of Ávila. She, too, emphasized the role of evocative images as a source of themes that helped discipline one's mind.[208] Hence, similarly to Mieleszko's and Morsztyn's poetic adaptations, the Carmelite *Pragnienia Dusze pobożnej* also tends to emphasize the visuality of the analyzed representations, directly pointing one's attention to the illustration pasted into the codex (II, 4.8): "Learn this, so as not to be upset with the instruments with which the Lord inflicts punishment on you and exercises his justice. See that the Lord's hand strikes you, albeit disguised in the form of another person and concealing his own visage."

Unlike the poets who wrote their translations with Princess Radziwiłł in mind, Zadzikowa readily referred to the technical aspect of spiritual exercises.

---

208   Teresa of Ávila, *Księgi duchowne* (Kraków: Balcer Śmieszkowic, 1664), 1:183.

The Carmelite author not only practiced meditation on a daily basis but also taught it to novices and laypeople.[209] She was keenly aware how effective memory, reason, and will were as tools helping one ponder over God's mysteries. In chapter II, 12, dedicated to the search for the concealed Bridegroom, Zadzikowa notes that only meditation founded on the three mental faculties can lead one to recognize Jesus's presence. In the teachings administered to novices who had trouble focusing on mental prayer, she pointed out that during meditation, reason must not be allowed to consider temporal things prompted by memory, and the will must not be inflamed with anyone other than God, otherwise Satan can turn prayer into a wellspring of sin.[210] Zadzikowa elaborated on this theme in one of the chapters of *Pragnienia Dusze pobożnej*, where she explained that it is precisely by taking over the three mental faculties that Satan gets one entangled in his web (I, 9.4).

The Carmelite adaptation of *Pia desideria* was penned by a consummate writer. The author's literary ambitions are demonstrated by her deliberate stylistic procedures. She eagerly flaunted her synonymy prowess to the reader—"**vanity, hollowness, fickleness, and insignificance** of worldly things" (I, 14.1), "shoots out words of love [...], **praises, blesses, honors, exalts, glorifies, recommends**" (III, 11.1). In order to underscore the sacred paradoxes, Zadzikowa also employed multiple oxymorons: "I am already satiated with **privation in affluence**, with **merriment sorrowful** and contrived, with **infamous fame**. Satiated is my Soul with **false brethren** and **hostile friends**" (III, 7.12).

Based on Hugo's exegetical excerpts, Zadzikowa created an adaptation designed to shape the inner life of Discalced Carmelite nuns. Although her work is evocative of a cento, as it combines a translation of the original text with authorial parts and works of different provenance (poetic quotations, monastic rule, meditation on the passion of Christ), each chapter nonetheless retains coherent and purposeful argumentation. As such, Zadzikowa's makes for one of the most ambitiously devised and intriguing Polish adaptations of *Pia desideria*.

6   Conclusions

6.1   *Literary Circulations: Oppositions and Interpenetrations*
6.1.1   Breaking Barriers
In analyzing the nature of the reception of *Pia desideria*, I highlighted its distinct tendencies toward a broadening of readership across denominations and

---

209   Gil, "Nauki o życiu zakonnym," 78, 89, 90, 98, 105–8.
210   Gil, "Nauki o życiu zakonnym," 106–7.

gender. These predilections are fully corroborated by the diverse nature of the literary adaptations of Hugo's collection.

In addition to the adaptations drafted with the Discalced Carmelite nuns in mind, there were translations by lay authors, addressed to a broad spectrum of readers, including both consecrated persons and those unaffiliated with the institutional church. Lacki's and Żaba's translations demonstrate that, from the mid-seventeenth century onward, *Pia desideria* was read by Polish magnates whose theological knowledge usually did not go beyond what they picked up at a Sunday sermon and who regarded their translational ventures as a pious work that, along with charitable deeds, would earn them salvation. With respect to the reception of *Pia desideria* among the laity, also signifi-cant is the case of the poets writing for Princess Radziwiłł, of whom the first (Mieleszko) was a Jesuit chaplain, while the second (Morsztyn) was a layman.

In the Polish adaptations of Hugo's volume, the least visible tendency is that toward an interdenominational reception. Among the authors seeking to introduce *Pia desideria* emblems to native readers, only one—the Unitarian Zbigniew Morsztyn—was non-Catholic. The first publisher of Morsztyn's emblems, Jan Dürr-Durski (1902–69), a researcher fascinated by the poetry of the Polish Brethren (in 1948, he published an anthology of the poetry of the Polish Arians)—underscored the links between Morsztyn's emblems and Unitarian ideology, identifying certain poems in the collection (1–6, 100, 101) as, in his opinion, written "in a state of severe mental depression" after Morsztyn's forced emigration to the Duchy of Prussia.[211]

One such poem is a subscription written to the equivalent of an engraving in *Pia desideria* (iii, 7). In it, the lyrical subject laments his living among the god-less who lie in wait for his life, so that there is no place where he can feel safe (3, vv. 1–10). This paragraph can be understood literally, as Dürr-Durski pro-posed; however, it does not negate the fact that the poet intended the meaning of his collection to be universal. In touching on the subject of earthly exile in several emblems, Morsztyn was bitterly aware of how harsh the fate of a refugee can be, but he transformed this awareness into a Christian longing for a heavenly homeland. Commissioned by a Catholic woman, the collection of poetic subscriptions to engravings collected by a Catholic monk never once accentuates Arian themes. The poet focused exclusively on the elements with which his magnate patron would be able to identify.

Conversely, the Polish translations of *Pia desideria* clearly attest to its female reception. Most of the adaptations discussed in this monograph were dedi-cated to women from princely and magnate families. Mieleszko and Morsztyn

---

211   Zbigniew Morsztyn, *Muza domowa*, ed. Jan Dürr-Durski (Warsaw: Państwowy Instytut Wydawniczy, 1954), 1:55.

inscribed their collections to Princess Katarzyna Radziwiłł. Lacki intended to dedicate his translation to the king's mother, Gryzelda Wiśniowiecka, eventually inscribing the volume to Konstancja Krystyna Wielopolska after Wiśniowiecka's passing. The 1744 edition of Żaba's translation carried a dedication to the grand camp leader of Lithuania, Ignacy Ogiński, and his wife Helena.

Also significant are the links between the handwritten copies of Polish adaptations and nunneries. A copy of the original redaction of Mieleszko's collection was transcribed by a Benedictine nun from the Sandomierz convent. The surviving annotations made by the nuns suggest their humble reading of the codex and their far-reaching identification with the lyrical heroine. A copy of *Wzdychania pobożne* has been preserved by the library of the Discalced Carmelite Nuns of Kraków, along with a strip of paper that served as a bookmark, which bears cross-references to commentaries on emblem III, 6 on the obverse, while the reverse contains a note by an anonymous Carmelite nun casting herself as an unworthy slave of the Virgin Mary, requesting that she intercede for the absolution of her sins. The copy of *Strzały serdeczne* was drafted by the Discalced Carmelite nun Agnieszka Konstancja of Lord Jesus the Lamb. The same copyist also transcribed the Lublin copy of *Pragnienia Dusze pobożnej*. Its subsequent owners included the magnate Elżbieta Febronia Koniecpolska and then the Benedictine convent in Lviv. Another copy of *Pragnienia Dusze pobożnej* was drawn up for the Discalced Carmelite nuns of the Warsaw convent. An anonymous translation of elegy III, 6 from an adaptation of the *Cor Iesu amanti sacrum* cycle addressed to nuns has been preserved as a copy currently kept at the Poor Clares' monastery in Stary Sącz (the codex formerly belonged to the Benedictine nunnery in Staniątki) and the Norbertine nuns in Imbramowice. Adaptations of *Pia desideria* were readily reproduced and read by nuns, attesting to its lively female reception.

It is worth noting that Hugo's volume spurred women to seize the pen in an era when Polish women very rarely engaged in literary creativity. In the West, spiritual women authors trying their hand at adapting Hugo's work, although few in number, were not an oddity. Cases in point include the Austrian Protestant poet Catharina Regina von Greiffenberg (1633–94) and her *Geburtsbetrachtungen* (Birth reflections),[212] and the first part of *L'ame amante de Son Dieu* (Soul loving its God) (J.694/F.407) by the French mystic Jeanne-Marie Bouvier de la

---

212   Cristina M. Pumplun, "Die gottliebende Seele und ihr Wegbereiter: Catharina Regina von Greiffenbergs *Geburtsbetrachtungen* (1678) und der Einfluß der Embleme der *Pia desideria* Herman Hugos s.j. (1624)," in *Brückenschläge: Eine barocke Festgabe für Ferdinand van Ingen*, ed. Martin Bircher and Guillaume van Gemert (Amsterdam: Rodopi, 1995), 211–31.

Motte-Guyon (1648–1717).[213] In the Polish–Lithuanian state, women's adaptations were only conceivable in cloistered settings.

The numerous group of prominent Polish lay writers of the seventeenth century included only three women authors. Two of them—Anna Memorata (c.1615–c.1645), daughter of a Bohemian pastor, and Sophia Anna Corbiniani di Bernhardi (d. before 1689), wife of the royal surgeon at the Vasa court—wrote exclusively Latin poems, and it is not known whether, or to what extent, they knew Polish. The third, Anna Zbąska née Stanisławska (1651/54–1700/1), was the author of a poetic autobiography from 1685 in which she recounted her three marriages. At the time, one could find many more women writers across Polish nunneries. Female congregations fostered the intellectual formation of nuns and were able to stimulate their creativity. The Discalced Carmelite nuns excelled in this department. The first Polish spiritual autobiography, short ascetic texts, and prayers were penned by the Discalced Carmelite nun Mother Teresa of Jesus (Marianna Marchocka [1603–52]).[214] This religious congregation also included authors of religious songs, Sisters Eufrazja of St. Casimir (Helena Sanguszkowa [d.1679]) and Paula Maria of Jesus (Helena Tekla Lubomirska [1622–87]), whose work is still pending recognition among literary historians.

Another prolific Carmelite nun, whose body of writing ranks second only to Marchocka's abundant oeuvre, was Zadzikowa.[215] It is to her writing temperament we owe the creation of the original adaptation of *Pragnienia Dusze pobożnej*. Another nun was the likely author of the four verses inscribed on the copies of Cornelis I Galle's (1576–1650) engravings, while still another wrote an adaptation of *Na słowa "Psalmu siedmdziesiątego wtórego" przydatek*, which included a Polish translation of Hugo's elegies. Compared with the rachitic contribution of women to the creation of Polish literary texts in the seventeenth century, the nuns' participation in adapting *Pia desideria* for the Polish audience can be regarded as massive.

6.1.2   Elitist and Egalitarian Circulation: Manuscripts versus Prints
During the baroque period, the number of printing houses in the territories of the Polish–Lithuanian Commonwealth steadily increased (with a short

---

213   Agnès Guiderdoni-Bruslé, "*L'ame amante de Son Dieu* by Madame Guyon (1717): Pure Love between Antwerp, Paris, and Amsterdam, at the Crossroads of Orthodoxy and Heterodoxy," in *The Low Countries as a Crossroads of Religious Beliefs*, ed. Arie Jan Gelderblom, Jan L. de Jong, and Marc van Vaeck (Leiden: Brill, 2004), 297–318.

214   Teresa od Jezusa (Marianna Marchocka), *Autobiografia mistyczna i inne pisma*, ed. Czesław Gil (Kraków: Wydawnictwo Karmelitów Bosych, 2010).

215   Czesław Gil, *Słownik polskich karmelitanek bosych 1612–1914* (Kraków: Wydawnictwo Karmelitów Bosych, 1999), 63.

hiatus caused by the destruction during the Polish–Swedish War of 1655–60, although these losses were quickly mitigated); consequently, the number of published titles also grew significantly. And yet, the most interesting literary works created at the time were preserved in the form of unauthorized copies. The reasons for the phenomenon that caused the seventeenth century to be referred to in Poland as "The Age of Manuscripts" can be traced to a change in the authors' approach to literary creation. With the printing press in mind, official texts were founded primarily on occasional, religious, or utilitarian premises, while works independent of panegyric requirements were created for oneself and one's nearest circle.[216]

One notable example of the above tendency is the work of Morsztyn, who collected his poems in a manuscript tellingly titled *Muza domowa*. In the accompanying preface, the poet clarified that he had written poetry to satisfy his own literary urges. The codex also included his emblems. Owners of similar manuscript collections, the so-called *silvae rerum*, copied borrowed texts of varied nature and provenance. They were intended for personal use, and the private manuscripts that contained them enabled readers to engage them intimately.

The circulation of handwritten texts also operated among consecrated persons, although the mechanisms that governed it are as yet poorly recognized. Their specific features include the free flow of texts between the convents of different orders, although they rarely entered lay circulation; and the fact that in women's convents the copyists were women, who selected the repertoire of circulating texts to serve their own needs, a practice that was virtually unheard of outside the convents in the seventeenth century.

The distribution channels of manuscripts and printed texts were radically different. Apart from the editions of Lacki's and Żaba's translations, all other evidence concerning the textual reception of *Pia desideria* is strictly elitist in nature. Mieleszko's and Morsztyn's adaptations, though dedicated to Princess Radziwiłł, did not live to see their publication at her behest, despite both poets' high hopes. Today, we know these two texts only because their authors took due care to distribute them in the form of handwritten copies.

Similarly, copies of Carmelite adaptations were intended for a narrow audience. In the case of dated copies of Zadzikowa's *Pragnienia Dusze pobożnej*, it is even possible to quote the exact size of the target group: the Carmelite congregation in Lublin, dedicated to the Immaculate Conception of the Blessed Virgin Mary, composed of sixteen nuns in 1662, while the Warsaw convent in

---

216   Adam Karpiński, "The Consequences of "The Age of Manuscripts": The Reconstruction of an Era," *Teksty drugie: Special Issue* 2 (2016): 68–83.

1697 was populated by twenty sisters.[217] If the Lublin copy got outside the convent, it was only to become the property of a single lay woman reader for a while. In the eighteenth century, it could again be used by a more numerous group of female users: the convent of Latin Benedictine nuns in Lviv at the time was made up of about forty nuns.

At present, researchers are primarily drawn to the Morsztyn and Mieleszko translations, outstanding in terms of their literary value, along with the recently discovered Carmelitan adaptations; one should remember, however, that in the seventeenth century said versions were unknown to broader audiences.

A different model of reception was shaped by the printed medium. Each successive edition of the book, which in the seventeenth and eighteenth centuries usually amounted to several hundred copies, significantly expanded its prospective audience. Therefore, the reception of *Pia desideria* was dominated by the editions of Lacki's and Żaba's translations. Released in a total of five editions, they were a product intended for a mass audience. Provenance notes on the surviving copies or inventories of old book collections indicate that the prints available on the book market for more than eighty years reached diverse reading groups. The numerous audiences interacting with these translations saw Hugo exclusively as a Jesuit lyric poet who set the standard for modern elegies with religious themes.

6.2   *Heterogeneity of* Pia desideria *in the Context of Its Different Reception Paths*

I have discussed the main reasons behind the popularity of Hugo's emblems. Among other things, they were favored on account of their structure. The model of the four-piece emblem proposed by the Jesuit author consisted of a biblical inscription and three different variations on its theme: exegetical, poetic, and graphic. The book was never translated into Polish in its entirety. The heterogeneous nature of the pieces provoked adaptors to focus on the element of the *emblema quadruplex* (fourfold emblem) that seemed the most appealing to a specific category of readers. The elegies primarily delighted lay audiences; excerpts from exegetical works proved crucial to the collection's reception among nuns; the iconographic solutions of the engravings attracted lay and consecrated readers alike. These three distinct reception models dominated the literary reception of *Pia desideria* in the Polish–Lithuanian state.

The Polish adaptations of *Pia desideria* cannot always be precisely dated. However, the dates that we do know point to a clear trend: after three decades

---

217   Grześkowiak, Gwioździk, and Nowicka-Struska, *Karmelitańskie adaptacje* Pia desideria, 66–67.

since the *editio princeps*, with nearly twenty Latin editions having saturated the publishing market, proper care was taken to bring *Pia desideria* also to those audiences that did not know Latin. The first stage of this process fell in the period between 1657 and 1671 and tapped into the second wave of revived interest in Hugo's emblematic volume. In 1657, Mieleszko drafted the final redaction of the adaptation based on an exegesis of the engravings, mentioning a planned translation of Hugo's elegies in the redaction's dedication. There is no certainty that this information is true, but by the 1660s such a translation had already been written by Lacki, and it was ready for print by 1671. The clean copy of an adaptation addressed to the Discalced Carmelites, which contained excerpts from exegetical works collected in *Pia desideria*, dates back to 1662. The translation known as *Strzały serdeczne* was produced before 1669. As can be seen in the earliest period of the Dutch collection's assimilation into Polish, although the adaptations focused on selected elements of the original collection, none of those elements was favored.

6.3   *Projected Models of Reception*
The diversity of reception paths is a testament to the validity of Hugo's decision: the complex form of *emblema quadruplex* invited a variety of fragmentary interpretations. Combining various components of emblems with the different needs of the target groups to which the respective adaptations were addressed resulted in a wider palette of literary reception models.

6.3.1   Meditative Readings
During the emergence of the first Polish adaptations of *Pia desideria*, methodical meditation was the predominant model of mental prayer. Thanks to the numerous translations and authorial collections of meditations produced in Polish, it was widely practiced by consecrated and laypeople alike, Catholics and Evangelicals, and its principles had long permeated poetry penned by the likes of Grochowski, a priest under the influence of the Jesuits, and Kasper Twardowski (1593–after 1631), an alumnus of the Jesuit sodality.

Not surprisingly, the reception of *Pia desideria* was dominated by the meditative model of reading. Since Hugo's elegies did not highlight the pattern of Ignatian spiritual exercises, Polish meditative adaptations routinely ignored their lyrical plane. Mieleszko and Morsztyn replaced Hugo's poems with their own subscriptions, in which they accorded the engravings the status of *compositio loci*. Their poems were intended to aid the reader in the mental prayer focused on the emblematic engravings, while the poets acted as spiritual guides of religious retreats, from the Sandomierz Benedictine nuns, who were friends of Mieleszko, to the lay readers of Morsztyn's subscriptions of the emblems, or Princess Katarzyna Radziwiłł, to whom both poets dedicated their respective collections.

Although the poetics of Zadzikowa's *Pragnienia Dusze pobożnej* is different, the reading model she proposed was also heavily influenced by the way of meditating. In the successive chapters, the author focused on the presentation of the engravings (*repraesentatio*), the consideration of their pictorial details (*consideratio*), and the final acts of will (*oratio*). Unlike the poetic cycles dedicated to Princess Radziwiłł, the adaptation addressed to nuns was subordinated to a greater extent to the prayerful form. Most of the woman protagonist's statements are directly addressed to God, which resulted in a continued emphasis on her sinfulness while also exposing the personal spiritual dimension of the text.

6.3.2   Artistic Readings

A translation of the greater part of Hugo's exegetical excerpts, *Westchnienia pobożne*, is perhaps the only adaptation among those accounted for in the present book whose creator may have had the ambition to appeal to the reader solely by means of philological fidelity. All the other adaptations are artistic in nature. The translational choices made by Lacki, Żaba, and the anonymous author in their respective translations of Hugo's elegies were dictated not only by compliance with the prevailing rules of translation but also by aesthetic considerations. Each of these authors strove for their translation to be equivalent to the original as a poetic work. In a similar vein, Mieleszko's and Morsztyn's rhymed subscriptions were also subordinated to lyrical artistry. An ornamental style, consciously employing artistic means of expression, likewise ranked among the overriding goals of the translator of *Strzały serdeczne* and the woman author of *Pragnienia Dusze pobożnej*.

The authors of the aforementioned adaptations were aware of the importance carried by the religious content addressed in the original. However, none was content with merely rendering them in their native language but instead wished to craft an artistic product whose aesthetic qualities matched the stature of its message in grandeur.

6.3.3   Spiritual Romance

Although Lacki was aware of the connections between Hugo's volume and meditative practice, in his 1671 preface addressed to Wiśniowiecka he proposed a different reading model. Lacki took advantage of the fact that the main characters of the collection are connected by a love relationship, full of passion, albeit subordinated to pious eroticism. In order to highlight this aspect, he did not use his translation of the elegies but instead relied on an exegesis of the

engravings and the attendant Latin inscriptions. This allowed him to accentu-
ate the adventurous and erotic theme, whose telling he styled after fashionable romances.

The translator thus met the expectations of his women readers, who were
hungry not only for spiritual content but also for a love plot. The romance key
he proposed for reading *Pia desideria* must have found many enthusiasts. Here
is eloquent proof thereof. The first printing of Lacki's translation was in the
possession of Bydgoszcz municipal judge Grabski, who kept it in his library. In
a book inventory, next to this very item, Grabski recorded lending the volume
to his wife. An identical annotation in this inventory marked the Polish translation of Torquato Tasso's (1544–95) *Gerusalemme liberata* (Jerusalem liberated),
which portrayed a crusade against the backdrop of elaborate love plots and
was read as a spiritual romance, as well as Stanisław Herakliusz Lubomirski's
Tobiasz wyzwolony (Tobias liberated),[218] which constitutes a paraphrase of the
biblical book of Tobias, in which the romance theme likewise plays a prominent role. Lacki's *Pobożne pragnienia* was apparently assimilated in a similar
fashion by Ms. Grabska.

If lay readers were able to interpret the text of *Pia desideria* in the above fashion, this was all the more true for nuns, who considered themselves betrothed
to Christ and celebrated the ceremony of monastic vows as mystical nuptials.
Their imperative to explore the mysteries of the *unio mystica*, with the Polish
version of Hugo's work in hand, was decidedly stronger. The distribution of
handwritten copies of *Wzdychania pobożne*, *Strzały serdeczne*, and *Pragnienia
Dusze pobożnej*, compiled for the Discalced Carmelite nuns, as well as the frequent occurrence of Lacki's and Żaba's translations in the book collections of
nunneries, serves as the best evidence in this regard.

6.3.4   Exegetical Readings
The three Polish adaptations of excerpts from the works of the doctors of the
church, which Hugo included in *Pia desideria*, are a recent discovery. Earlier
on, it seemed that Polish authors were only interested in erudite elegies or
emblematic images, since the popular adaptations omitted the component
that occupied the most space in the *Pia desideria* volume. It turns out, however,
that the excerpts did arouse keen interest, but among professional audiences
(i.e., the Discalced Carmelite nuns), whose reading of Hugo's collection focused
on the statements by holy authors whose writings were the key to comprehend
the inspired words of the Bible.

---

218   Paulina Buchwald-Pelcowa, "Inwentarz biblioteki Jana Kazimierza Grabskiego," 353, 356.

In addition to the translations of two versions of Hugo's exegetical excerpts—the full and the abridged one—there is also Zadzikowa's adaptation. She transformed the original collection of excerpts into a non-narrative text with a distinct, prayerful texture, into which she skillfully wove biblical quotations, passages from the works of the doctors of the church (or those that purported to be such), items from the monastic rule, and stanzas of Carmelite poetry. The result was an original work of a formative nature, which dashingly processed themes adopted from *Pia desideria*.

The attractiveness of Hugo's collection not only caused its Latin version to be eagerly read across the Polish–Lithuanian state but also sparked a number of translations into Polish, inviting the emergence of new works created on the basis of the Latin original and inspiring painting decorations in numerous temples. As a result of these activities, *Pia desideria* became the foremost emblem book, which for nearly a century and a half in various literary and artistic incarnations guided the citizens of the Polish–Lithuanian Commonwealth to abandon their sins, harden themselves in Christian virtues, and attain union with God.

Bibliography

The bibliography does not include editions of the original text of *Pia desideria*.

Primary Sources

Alciato, Andrea. *Emblematum libellus*. Paris: Chrestien Wechel, 1534.

Augustyn, Aureliusz. *Ksiąg pięcioro*. Translated by [Jan Aland]. Vilnius: Akademia Jezuicka, 1617.

Bielicki, Stanisław. *Matka publicznych żalów* [...], *Katarzyna z Sobieszyna Radziwiłłowa* [...], *pogrzebowym kazaniem opłakana*. Warsaw: Szkoła Pijarska, 1695.

Chmielowski, Benedykt. *Nowe Ateny*. 2nd ed. Vol. 1. Part 1. Lwów: Kolegium Jezuickie, 1754.

Drużbicki, Kasper. *Droga doskonałości chrześcijańskiej na trzy części rozłożona*. Kalisz: Kolegium Jezuickie, 1665.

Drużbicki, Kasper. "Rekolekcje sandomierskie." Edited by Jan Maria Szymusiak, *Sacrum Poloniae Millenium* 11 (1965): 615–60.

Fałęcki, Hilarion. *Wojsko serdecznych nowo rekrutowanych na większą chwałę Boską afektów*. Poznań: Drukarnia Akademicka, 1746.

Gil, Czesław. "Nauki o życiu zakonnym m. Anny Stobieńskiej oraz m. Teresy Barbary Zadzikowej, karmelitanek bosych." *Nasza przeszłość* 105 (2006): 43–116.

Gil, Czesław ed. *Żywot matki Barbary od Najśw[iętszego] Sakramentu (Zadzikowej), karmelitanki bosej (1609–1670)*. Kraków: Wydawnictwo Karmelitów Bosych, 2013.

Grześkowiak, Radosław, Jolanta Gwioździk, and Anna Nowicka-Struska. *Karmelitańskie adaptacje Pia desideria Hermana Hugona z XVII i XVIII w.* Warsaw: Neriton, 2020.

Guiderdoni-Bruslé, Agnès, and Aline Smeesters, eds. *Emblèmes et poésies des Pieux désirs de Herman Hugo (Anvers–Paris, 1627)*. Turnhout: Brepols, 2013.

Hugo, Herman. *Pia desideria or Divine Addresses in Three Books*. Englished by Edm[und] Arwaker. London: Henry Bonwicke, 1686.

Hugo, Herman. *Pobożne pragnienia*. Translated by Aleksander Teodor Lacki. Kraków: Dziedzice Krzysztofa Schedla, 1673.

Hugo, Herman. *Pobożne pragnienia*. Translated by Aleksander Teodor Lacki. Kraków: Nakład Jerzego Romualda Schedla, 1697.

Hugo, Herman. *Pobożne pragnienia*. Translated by Aleksander Teodor Lacki. Kraków: Nakład Jerzego Romualda Schedla, 1737.

Hugo, Herman. *Pobożne pragnienia*. Translated by [Jan Kazimierz Żaba]. [Supraśl: Drukarnia Bazylianów], 1744.

Hugo, Herman. *Pobożne pragnienia*. Translated by Bonifacy Ostrzykowski. Warsaw: Księża Misjonarze, 1843.

Hugo, Herman. *Pobożne żądania*. Translated by Jan Kościesza Żaba. Vilnius: Akademia Jezuicka, 1754.

Kochowski, Wespazjan. *Niepróżnujące próżnowanie*. Kraków: Wojciech Górecki, 1674.

Komoniecki, Andrzej. *Chronografia albo Dziejopis żywiecki*. Edited by Stanisław Grodziski and Irena Dwornicka. Żywiec: Towarzystwo Miłośników Ziemi Żywieckiej, 1987.

Królikowski, Janusz, ed. *"Serce me daję": Archiwum Klarysek w Starym Sączu 2*. Tarnów: Biblos, 2012.

Lacki, Aleksander Teodor. *Pobożne pragnienia*. Edited by Krzysztof Mrowcewicz. Warsaw: Wydawnictwo IBL, 1997.

Melecius, Michał Brokard, trans. *Sposób mądrego i dobrego życia na świecie [...] od ś[więtego] Bernata*. Kraków: Franciszek Cezary, 1630.

Mikołaj, Mieleszko. *Emblematy*. Edited by Radosław Grześkowiak and Jakub Niedźwiedź. Warsaw: Neriton, 2010.

Morsztyn, Zbigniew. *Emblemata*. Edited by Janusz and Paulina Pelcowie. Warsaw: Neriton, 2001.

Morsztyn, Zbigniew. *Muza domowa*. Edited by Jan Dürr-Durski. Vol. 1. Warsaw: Państwowy Instytut Wydawniczy, 1954.

Pelcowie, Janusz and Paulina Pelcowie, eds. *"Miłości Boskiej i ludzkiej skutki różne" wraz z siedemnastowieczną polską wersją tekstów do "Amoris Divini et humani effectus varii"*. Warsaw: Neriton, 2000.

Pochodnia duchowna [...] wyjęta z ksiąg ś[więtego] Bonawentury. Kraków: Mikołaj Lob, 1609.

Pontanus, Jacobus [Jakob Spanmüller]. *Institutio poetica*. Cologne: Sumptibus Bernardi Gualtheri, 1605.

Puente, Luis de la. *Rozmyślania o tajemnicach wiary naszej*. Translated by Jan Węgrzynkowic. Vol. 1. Jarosław: Jan Szeliga, 1621.

Quarles, Francis. Emblemes (*1635*) *and* Hieroglyphikes of the Life of Man (*1638*). Edited by Karl Josef Höltgen and John Horden. Hildesheim: Georg Olms, 1993.

Reguła i konstytucyje zakonnic karmelitanek bosych. Kraków: Wdowa i dziedzice Andrzeja Piotrkowczyka, 1635.

Rollenhagen, Gabriel. *Nucleus emblematum selectissimorum*. Vol. 1. Cologne: Crispijn van de Passe, 1611.

Sarbiewski, Maciej Kazimierz. *O poezji doskonałej, czyli Wergiliusz i Homer* [*De perfecta poesi, sive Vergilius et Homerus*]. Translated by Marian Plezia, edited by Stanisław Skimina. Wrocław: Zakład Narodowy im. Ossolińskich, 1954.

Sucquet, Antoine. *Via vitae aeternae*. Antwerp: Typis Martini Nutii, 1620.

Świrski, Kazimierz Tomasz Saława. *Honor laureis poeticis coronatus seu epigrammata in proceres Poloniae Senatus*. Lublin: Kolegium Jezuickie, 1749.

Veen, Otto van. *Amoris Divini emblemata*. Antwerp: Martin Nuyts, 1615.

Veen, Otto van. *Q. Horati Flacci emblemata*. Antwerp: Hieronymus Verdussen, 1607.

Secondary Sources

Adams, Alison, Stephen Rawles, and Alison Saunders. *A Bibliography of French Emblem Books of the Sixteenth and Seventeenth Centuries*. Vols. 1–2. Geneva: Librairie Droz, 1999–2000.

Backer, Augustin de, Aloys de Backer, and Carlos Sommervogel, eds. *Bibliothèque des écrivains de la Compagnie de Jésus*. Vol. 4. Liège: Grandmont-Donders, 1893.

Barłowska, Maria. "Litteraria w rękopiśmiennym inwentarzu ksiąg Krzysztofa Tomasza Drohojowskiego." *Rocznik przemyski* 48, no. 2 (2012): 273–84.

Black, Lynette C. "Popular Devotional Emblematics. A Comparison of Sucquet's *Le chemin de la vie eternele* and Hugo's *Les pieux desirs*." *Emblematica* 9, no. 1 (1995): 1–20.

Bloemendal, Jan. "Een emblematicus en zijn inspiratie: De bronnen van Otho Vaenius' *Amoris divini emblemata*, Antwerpen 1615; Ontlening en adaptie." *Tijdschrift Voor Nederlandse Taal-en Letterkunde* 118 (2002): 273–87.

Buchwald-Pelcowa, Paulina. *Emblematy w drukach polskich i Polski dotyczących XVI–XVIII wieku: Bibliografia*. Wrocław: Zakład Narodowy im. Ossolińskich, 1981.

Buchwald-Pelcowa, Paulina. "Emblematyka w polskich kolegiach jezuickich." In *Artes atque humaniora: Studia Stanislao Mossakowski sexagenario dicata*, edited by Andrzej Rottermund et al., 169–79. Warsaw: Instytut Sztuki PAN, 1998.

Buchwald-Pelcowa, Paulina. "Inwentarz biblioteki Jana Kazimierza Grabskiego z 1691 roku." In *Historia literatury i historia książki. Studia nad książką i literaturą od średniowiecza po wiek XVIII*, 341–58. Kraków: Universitas, 2005.

Buchwald-Pelcowa, Paulina. "Typologia polskich książek emblematycznych." *Barok* 3, no. 1 (1996): 59–75.

Campa, Pedro F. "The Spanish and Portuguese Adaptations of Herman Hugo's *Pia desideria*." In *Emblematic Perceptions: Essays in Honor of William S. Heckscher on the Occasion of his Ninetieth Birthday*, edited by Peter M. Daly and Daniel S. Russell, 43–60. Baden-Baden: V. Koerner, 1997.

Carvalho, José Adriano de Freitas. "As lágrimas e as setas: Os *Pia desideria* de Herman Hugo, S.J. em Portugal." *Via spiritus* 2 (1995): 169–201.

Chévre, Marie. "*Pia desideria* illustrés par Boëce de Bolswert." *Gutenberg Jahrbuch* 41 (1966): 291–99.

Chrzanowski, Tadeusz. "Kościół w Starym Mieście pod Dzierzgoniem p.w. św. Apostołów Piotra i Pawła: Emblematyka w służbie protestantyzmu." In *Sztuka Prus XIII–XVIII w.*, edited by Agnieszka Bojarska, 199–226. Toruń: Wydawnictwo UMK, 1994.

Cubrzyńska-Leonarczyk, Maria. *Katalog druków supraskich*. Warsaw: Biblioteka Narodowa, 1996.

Czerniatowicz, Janina, and Czesław Mazur. *Recepcja antyku chrześcijańskiego w Polsce: Materiały bibliograficzne*. Vol. 1, *XV–XVIII w.* Part 1, *Autorzy i teksty*. Lublin: TNKUL, 1978.

Daly, Peter M., and G. Richard Dimler. *The Jesuit Series*. Vol. 3. Toronto: University of Toronto Press, 2002.

Daly, Peter M., and G. Richard Dimler. "The New Edition of Herman Hugo's *Pia desideria* in Polish and Recent Hugo Scholarship." *Emblematica* 12 (2002): 351–60.

Dambre, Oscar. "Nabeschouwingen over *Pia desideria* (1624) en *Goddelijcke wenschen* (1629)." *Spiegel der Letteren* 2 (1958): 59–65.

Dekoninck, Ralph. "The Circulation of Images." In Emblemata sacra: *Emblem Books from the Maurits Sabbe Library, Katholieke Universiteit Leuven*, edited by Ralph Dekoninck, Agnès Guiderdoni-Bruslé, and Marc van Vaeck, 31–36. Philadelphia: Saint Joseph's University Press, 2006.

Dietz, Feike. *Literaire levensaders: Internationale uitwisseling van woord, beeld en religie in de Republiek*. Hilversum: Verloren, 2012.

Dietz, Feike. "Media Literate Catholics: Seeing, Reading, and Writing in Early Modern Participatory Culture." *Authorship* 2 (2013): 1–22.

Dietz, Feike. "*Pia desideria* through Children's Eyes: The Eighteenth-Century Revival of *Pia desideria* in a Dutch Children's Book." *Emblematica* 17 (2009): 191–212.

Dietz, Feike. "Under the Cover of Augustine: Augustinian Spirituality and Catholic Emblems in the Seventeenth-Century Dutch Republic." In *Augustine beyond the Book: Intermediality, Transmediality, and Reception*, edited by Karla Pollmann and Meredith J. Gill, 167–94. Leiden: Brill, 2012.

Dietz, Feike, Els Stronks, and Katarzyna Zawadzka. "Rooms-katholieke *Pia desideria*: Bewerkingen in internationaal perspectief." *Internationale Neerlandistiek* 47, no. 3 (2009): 31–49.

Dimler, G. Richard. "Arwaker's Translation of the *Pia Desideria*. The Reception of a Continental Jesuit Emblem Book in Seventeenth-Century England." In *The English Emblem and the Continental Tradition*, edited by Peter M. Daly, 203–25. New York: AMS Press, 1988.

Dimler, G. Richard. "A Bibliographical Survey of Emblem Books Produced by Jesuit Colleges in the Early Society: Topography and Themes." *Archivum historicum Societatis Iesu* 48 (1979): 297–309.

Dimler, G. Richard. "Herman Hugo's *Pia desideria*." In Mundus emblematicus: *Studies in Neo-Latin Emblem Books*, edited by Karl A.E. Enenkel and Arnoud S.Q. Visser, 351–79. Turnhout: Brepols, 2003.

Dimler, G. Richard. "Jesuit Emblem Books: An Overview of Research Past and Present." In *Emblem Studies in Honour of Peter M. Daly*, edited by Michael Bath, Pedro F. Campa, and Daniel S. Russell, 63–122. Baden-Baden: V. Koerner, 2002.

Długosz, Józef. "Biblioteka klasztoru karmelitów bosych w Wiśniczu (1630–1649)." *Archiwa, biblioteki i muzea kościelne* 13 (1966): 91–169.

Długosz, Józef. "Księgozbiór Aleksandra Michała Lubomirskiego w świetle inwentarza z 1678 r." *Ze skarbca kultury* 23 (1972): 7–52.

Enenkel, Karl A.E. "Florentius Schoonhovius *Emblemata partim moralia, partim etiam civilia*: Text and Paratext." In *Emblems of the Low Countries: A Book Historical Perspective*, edited by Alison Adams and Marleen van der Weij, 129–47. Glasgow: Librairie Droz, 2003.

Estabridis, Ricardo. "Arte y vida mística: El alma y el amor divino en la pintura virreinal." *Revista del Museo Nacional* 50 (2010): 129–155.

Estabridis, Ricardo. "La cultura emblemática jesuita en una Casa de Ejercicios Espirituales para señoras limeñas." *Illapa* 8 (2011): 29–41.

Folguera, José Miguel Morales. "La celda del Padre Salamanca en el Convento de la Merced de Cuzco: Guia conceptual de la vida religiosa mercedaria en el altiplano peruano del setecientos." *Imago* 1 (2009): 79–97.

Gil, Czesław. *Słownik polskich karmelitanek bosych 1612–1914*. Kraków: Wydawnictwo Karmelitów Bosych, 1999.

Grześkowiak, Radosław. "Anonimowe dzieło emblematyczne na kanwie cyklu rycin *Cor Iesu amanti sacrum* Antonia Wierixa z drugiej połowy XVII stulecia." *Pamiętnik literacki* 104, no. 3 (2013): 217–30.

Grześkowiak, Radosław. "Polska recepcja *Pia desideria*: Typy odbioru religijnych zbiorów emblematycznych." In *Dialogi dzieł dawnych: Studia o intertekstualności literatury staropolskiej*, 169–218. Gdańsk: Wydawnictwo UG, 2018.

Grześkowiak, Radosław. "'Zwyczajem kawalerów ziemskich postępuje z nią Oblubieniec': Pierwotna dedykacja *Pobożnych pragnień* Aleksandra Teodora Lackiego jako autorski projekt lektury emblematów Hermana Hugona." *Pamiętnik literacki* 106, no. 1 (2015): 199–227.

Grześkowiak, Radosław, and Paul Hulsenboom. "Emblems from the Heart: The Reception of the *Cor Iesu amanti sacrum* Engravings Series in Polish and Netherlandish 17th-Century Manuscripts." *Werkwinkel* 10, no. 2 (2015): 131–54.

Grześkowiak, Radosław, and Jakub Niedźwiedź. "Unknown Polish Subscriptions to the Emblems of Otto van Veen and Herman Hugo: A Study on the Functioning of Western Religious Engravings in the Old-Polish Culture." *Terminus: Special Issue* 1 (2019): 1–29.

Grześkowiak, Radosław, Jolanta Gwioździk, and Anna Nowicka-Struska. *Karmelitańskie adaptacje* Pia desideria *Hermana Hugona z XVII i XVIII w.* Warsaw: Neriton, 2020.

Guiderdoni-Bruslé, Agnès. "*L'ame amante de Son Dieu* by Madame Guyon (1717): Pure Love between Antwerp, Paris and Amsterdam, at the Crossroads of Orthodoxy and Heterodoxy." In *The Low Countries as a Crossroads of Religious Beliefs*, edited by Arie Jan Gelderblom, Jan L. de Jong, and Marc van Vaeck, 297–318. Leiden: Brill, 2004.

Gurba, Stanisław. "Treści przedstawień emblematycznych na konfesjonałach w kościele św. Pawła w Sandomierzu." *Kronika diecezji sandomierskiej* 107, nos. 3/4 (2014): 243–51.

Hałoń, Joanna. "W poszukiwaniu źródeł inspiracji, czyli o dwóch polskich wersjach *Pia desideria* Hermana Hugona." *Roczniki humanistyczne* 50, no. 2 (2002): 127–60.

Hałoń, Joanna. "Wobec obrazu." *Zeszyty naukowe Katolickiego Uniwersytetu Lubelskiego* 46, nos. 1/2 (2003): 33–61.

Hanusiewicz, Mirosława. "Polskie barokowe przekłady i adaptacje *Glosy* św. Teresy z Avila." In *Barok polski wobec Europy: Sztuka przekładu*, edited by Alina Nowicka-Jeżowa and Marek Prejs, 241–57. Warsaw: Anta, 2005.

Hanusiewicz, Mirosława. *Święte i zmysłowe w poezji religijnej polskiego baroku.* Lublin: Wydawnictwo KUL, 1998.

Höltgen, Karl Josef. "Catholic Pictures versus Protestant Words? The Adaptation of the Jesuit Sources in Quarles's *Emblemes.*" *Emblematica* 9, no. 1 (1995): 221–38.

Höltgen, Karl Josef. "Emblem and Meditation: Some English Emblem Books and Their Jesuit Models." *Explorations in Renaissance Culture* 18 (1992): 58–66.

Höpel, Ingrid. "Antwerpen auf Eiderstedt: Ein Emblemzyklus nach Hermann Hugos *Pia Desideria* in St. Katharina, Katharinenheerd auf Eiderstedt, zwischen 1635 und 1650." *De zeventiende eeuw* 20 (2004): 322–42.

Höpel, Ingrid. "Change of Medium: From Book Graphics to Art in Sacred Space; With the Example of an Emblem-Cycle on a Church Gallery at Katharinenheerd." In *Das Emblem im Widerspiel von Intermedialität und Synmedialität*, edited by Johannes Köhler and Wolfgang Christian Schneider, 189–225. Hildesheim: Georg Olms, 2007.

Karkucińska, Wanda. *Anna z Sanguszków Radziwiłłowa (1676–1746): Działalność gospodarcza i mecenat.* Warsaw: Neriton, 2000.

Karpiński, Adam. "The Consequences of 'The Age of Manuscripts': The Reconstruction of an Era." *Teksty drugie: Special Issue* 2 (2016): 68–83.

Klimowska, Monika Anna. "Graficzne pierwowzory alegorycznych obrazów z opactwa sióstr benedyktynek w Staniątkach." In *Inspiracje grafiką europejską w sztuce polskiej: czasy nowożytne*, edited by Krystyna Moisan-Jabłońska and Katarzyna Ponińska, 129–44. Warsaw: Wydawnictwo UKSW, 2010.

Konečný, Lubomír. "The Rise and Fall of a Hero." In *Impossible Heroes: Icarus and Phaeton as the Emblematic Figures of Modern Man*, edited by Eva Bendová, Václav Hájek, Lubomír Konečný, and Ondřej Váša, 15–36. Prague: Národní galerie, 2020.

Kozieł, Andrzej. "Willmann i barbarzyńcy, czyli słów kilka o dekoracji malarskiej stropów z dawnego pałacu opatów lubiąskich w Moczydlnicy Klasztornej." In *Opactwo cystersów w Lubiążu i artyści*, edited by Andrzej Kozieł, 294–310. Wrocław: Wydawnictwo UWr, 2008.

Kroll, Walter. "*Poeta laureatus* Stefan Jaworski i emblematyka." *Terminus* 20, no. 2 (2018): 195–253.

Kwiatkowska-Frejlich, Lidia. *Funkcje potrydenckiej sztuki kościelnej: Nowożytny wystrój kościoła Brygidek w Lublinie.* Lublin: Wydawnictwo UMCS, 2009.

Landwehr, John. *Emblem and Fable Books Printed in the Low Countries 1542–1813: A Bibliography.* 3rd ed. Utrecht: HES, 1988.

Landwehr, John. *German Emblem Books 1531–1888: A Bibliography.* Utrecht: A.W. Sijthoff, 1972.

Leach, Mark Carter. "The Literary and Emblematic Activity of Herman Hugo, S.J. (1588–1629): A Dissertation." PhD diss., University of Delaware, 1979.

Małkus, Marta. "Malowane medytacje religijne inspirowane *Pia desideria* Hermana Hugo: Program ikonograficzny polichromii w kościele pw. św. Stanisława Biskupa i Męczennika oraz Wniebowzięcia NMP we Wschowie." In *Życie duchowe na ziemi wschowskiej i pograniczu wielkopolsko-śląskim*, edited by Marta Małkus and Kamila Szymańska, 241–59. Wschowa: Czas A.R.T., 2017.

Marcinowska, Maria. "Emblematy ze ścian dworu z Rdzawy w Sądeckim Parku Etnograficznym." *Rocznik sądecki* 37 (2009): 161–81.

Marcinowska, Maria. "Lubomirscy z linii wiśnickiej jako propagatorzy kultury w swoich włościach." *Zeszyty sądecko-spiskie* 3 (2008): 124–30.

Mödersheim, Sabine. "The Emblem in the Context of Architecture." In *Emblem Scholarship. Directions and Developments: a Tribute to Gabriel Hornstein*, ed. Peter M. Daly, 159–75. Turnhout: Brepols, 2005.

Monita, Rafał, and Andrzej Skorupa. *Nowy Targ: Kościół świętej Katarzyny Aleksandryjskiej.* Kraków: Astraia, 2012.

Monteiro, João Pedro. "Os *Pia desideria*, uma fonte iconográfica da azulejaria portuguesa do século XVIII." *Azulejo* 3/7 (1995/99): 61–70.

Mrowcewicz, Krzysztof. "'O miłości Bożej rozmyślanie': O *Emblematach* Zbigniewa Morsztyna." In *Literatura i kultura polska po "potopie"*, edited by Barbara Otwinowska, Janusz Pelc, and Barbara Falęcka, 153–64. Wrocław: Zakład Narodowy im. Ossolińskich, 1992.

Mrowcewicz, Krzysztof. *Trivium poetów polskich epoki baroku: klasycyzm—manieryzm—barok.* Warsaw: IBL, 2005.

Müller, Wolfgang J. "Die Emporenbilder von Katharinenheerd: Ein Beitrag zur Bildwelt des 17. Jahrhunderts in Schleswig-Holstein." *Nordelbingen* 40 (1971): 91–109.

Николаев, Сергей И. "Литературные занятия Ивана Максимовича." *Труды Отдела древнерусской литературы* 40 (1985): 385–99.

Noworyta-Kuklińska, Bożena. "Program ideowy malowideł zakrystii kościoła pw. Nawrócenia świętego Pawła Apostoła w Sandomierzu." In *Fides imaginem quaerens: Studia ofiarowane Księdzu Profesorowi Ryszardowi Knapińskiemu w siedemdziesiątą rocznicę urodzin*, edited by Aneta Kramiszewska, 151–70. Lublin: Werset, 2011.

Pelc, Janusz. *Zbigniew Morsztyn: Arianin i poeta.* Wrocław: Zakład Narodowy im. Ossolińskich, 1966.

Pfeiffer, Bogusław. "*Pobożne pragnienia* Aleksandra Teodora Lackiego: Pierwszy polski przekład utworu emblematycznego Hermana Hugona *Pia desideria*." *Ze skarbca kultury* 44 (1987): 9–52.

Pfeiffer, Bogusław. "'Zegar cudowny nieba': Symbolika przestrzeni w utworach Zbigniewa Morsztyna." *Acta Universitatis Wratislaviensis: Prace literackie* 42 (2003): 5–43.

Pietrzak, Jarosław. *Księżna dobrodziejka: Katarzyna z Sobieskich Radziwiłłowa (1634–1694).* Warsaw: Muzeum w Wilanowie, 2016.

Polman, Pontianus [Pontien], et al. "De *Pia desideria* va pater Herman Hugo S.J. (1624)." Supplement to *Mons Alvernae* 18 (1942–43).

Porteman, Karel. "Nieuwe gegevens over de drukgeschiedenis, de bronnen en de auteur van de embleembundel *Amoris divini et humani antipathia*." *Ons geestelijk erf* 49 (1975): 193–213.

Praz, Mario. *Studies in Seventeenth-Century Imagery.* Vol. 1. Rome: Edizioni di Storia e Letteratura, 1975.

Pumplun, Cristina M. "Die gottliebende Seele und ihr Wegbereiter: Catharina Regina von Greiffenbergs *Geburtsbetrachtungen* (1678) und der Einfluß der Embleme der *Pia desideria* Herman Hugos S.J. (1624)." In *Brückenschläge: Eine barocke Festgabe für Ferdinand van Ingen*, edited by Martin Bircher and Guillaume van Gemert, 211–31. Amsterdam: Rodopi, 1995.

Raspa, Anthony. "Arwaker, Hugo's *Pia desideria*, and Protestant Poetics." *Renaissance and Reformation* 24, no. 2 (2000): 63–74.

Reimbold, Ernst Thomas. "*Geistlische Seelenlust*: Ein Beitrag zur barocken Bildmeditation: Hugo Hermann, *Pia Desideria*, Antwerpen 1624." *Symbolon: Jahrbuch für Symbolforschung* N.F. 4 (1978): 93–161.

Rödter, Gabriele. "*Ordo naturalis* und meditative Struktur: Devotionslyrik im Kräftespiel von Emblematik, Rhetorik und Meditationspraxis dargelegt am Beispiel ausgewählter Kapitel der *Pia desideria* des Hermann Hugo S.J." In *Religion und Religiosität im Zeitalter des Barock*, in Verbindung mit Barbara Becker-Cantarino, Heinz Schilling, Walter Sparn, hrsg. Dieter Breuer, 2: 523–38. Wiesbaden: Harrassowitz, 1995.

Rödter, Gabriele. *Via piae animae: Grundlagenuntersuchung zur emblematischen Verknüpfung von Bild und Wort in den* Pia desideria *(1624) des Herman Hugo S.J. (1588–1629)*. Frankfurt am Main: Peter Lang, 1992.

Różycki, Edward. "Inwentarz książek lwowianina Ludwika Waleriana Alembeka z 1704 roku." *Roczniki biblioteczne* 40, nos. 1/2 (1996): 109–38.

Russell, Daniel S. "Claude Mignault, Erasmus, and Simon Bouquet: The Function of the Commentaries on Alciato's Emblems." In Mundus emblematicus: *Studies in Neo-Latin Emblem Books*, edited by Karl A.E. Enenkel and Arnoud S.Q. Visser, 17–32. Turnhout: Brepols, 2003.

Schilling, Michael. "Emblematik außerhalb des Buches." *Internationales Archiv für Sozialgeschichte der deutschen Literatur* 11 (1986): 149–74.

Schilling, Michael. "'Der rechte Teutsche Hugo': Deutschsprachige Übersetzungen und Bearbeitungen der *Pia Desideria* Hermann Hugos Jesuit." *Germanisch-romanische Monatsschrift* 70 (1989): 283–300.

Schuster, Kamila. "O autorstwie *Regestru ksiąg* z roku 1676 i ich właścicielu Krzysztofie Tomaszu Drohojowskim." *Ze skarbca kultury* 29 (1977): 43–61.

Skorupa, Andrzej. "*Pobożne pragnienia*: O obrazach z Frydmana i Nowego Targu." *Wierchy* 69 (2003): 166–72.

Stankiewicz, Aleksander. "Sanktuarium Matki Bożej Rychwałdzkiej: Na pograniczu tradycji kultu i odniesień do przeszłości w sztuce." In *Historyzm—tradycjonalizm—archaizacja: Studia z dziejów świadomości historycznej w średniowieczu i okresie nowożytnym*, edited by Marek Walczak, 234–48. Kraków: Societas Vistulana, 2015.

Stephen, Mary Wanda. "Do biografii i twórczości Zbigniewa Morsztyna." *Pamiętnik literacki* 54, no. 4 (1963): 415–42.

Szczęsny, Stanisław. "*Pia desideria* Hermana Hugona w bibliotece benedyktynek sandomierskich: Nieznany przekład polski." In *Literatura polskiego baroku w kręgu idei*, ed. Alina Nowicka-Jeżowa, Mirosława Hanusiewicz, and Adam Karpiński, 161–65. Lublin: Wydawnictwo KUL, 1995.

Szupieńko, Stanisław. "Mistyka oblubieńcza w programie dekoracji malarskiej kościoła poewangelickiego w Kościelcu koło Legnicy." In *Willmann i inni: Malarstwo, rysunek i grafika na Śląsku i w krajach ościennych w XVII i XVIII wieku*, edited by Andrzej Kozieł and Beata Lejman, 192–99. Wrocław: IHS Uniwersytetu Wrocławskiego, 2002.

Talbierska, Jolanta. *Grafika XVII wieku w Polsce: Funkcje, ośrodki, artyści, dzieła*. Warsaw: Neriton, 2011.

Treiderowa, Anna. "Ze studiów nad ilustracją wydawnictw krakowskich w wieku XVII (z drukarń: Piotrkowczyków, Cezarych, Szedlów i Kupiszów)." *Rocznik Biblioteki Polskiej Akademii Nauk w Krakowie* 14 (1968): 5–41.

van der Heyden, Jacob. *Pugillus facetiarum iconographicarum in studiosorum potissimum gratiam* [...]. Strasburg, 1618.

van Haeften, Benedictus. *Regia via crucis*. Antwerp: Officina Plantiniana, 1635.

Visser, Arnoud. "Commonplaces of Catholic Love: Otto van Veen, Michel Hoyer, and St Augustine between Humanism and the Counter-Reformation." In *Learned Love*, edited by Els Stronks and Peter Boot, with the assistance of Dagmar Stiebral, 33–48. The Hague: DANS, 2007.

Voisine-Jechova, Hana. "La visualisation ambiguë: Les emblèmes polonais de Morsztyn et leurs modèles." *Revue de littèrature comparèe* 64, no. 4 (1990): 689–703.

Welsh, David J. "Zbigniew Morsztyn's Poetry of Meditation." *Slavic and East European Journal* 9, no. 1 (1965): 56–61.

Wisłocki, Marcin. "From Emblem Books to Ecclesiastical Space: Emblems and Quasi-emblems in Protestant Churches on the Southern Coast of the Baltic Sea and Their Devotional Background." In *The Emblem in Scandinavia and the Baltic*, edited by Simon McKeown and Mara R. Wade, 279–84. Glasgow: Librairie Droz 2006.

Wisłocki, Marcin. "Hugo wędruje na wschód: Uwagi o recepcji *Pia desideria* Hermana Hugona w sztuce protestanckiej Europy Środkowej." *Quart* 15, no. 2 (2020): 17–33.

Wisłocki, Marcin. *Sztuka protestancka na Pomorzu 1535–1684*. Szczecin: Muzeum Narodowe, 2005.

Wiśniewski, Jan. *Historyczny opis kościołów, miast, zabytków i pamiątek w olkuskiem*. Mariówka Opoczyńska: Szkoła rzemieślnicza, 1933.

Wójcik, Dagmara Liliana. "Jezuicka mistyka w protestanckim wnętrzu: Ze studiów nad programem ideowym kościoła w Starym Mieście koło Dzierzgonia." In *Sztuka i dialog wyznań w XVI i XVII wieku*, edited by Jan Harasimowicz, 325–36. Warsaw: SHS, 2000.

Index

If you have any questions regarding this title, please contact:

Koninklijke Brill BV
Plantijnstraat 2
2321 JC Leiden
Email: info@brill.com

Batch number: 08427054